Deep Learning Quick Reference

Useful hacks for training and optimizing deep neural networks with TensorFlow and Keras

Mike Bernico

BIRMINGHAM - MUMBAI

Deep Learning Quick Reference

Commissioning Editor: Amey Varangaonkar
Acquisition Editor: Viraj Madhav
Content Development Editor: Varun Sony
Technical Editor: Dharmendra Yadav
Copy Editors: Safis Editing
Project Coordinator: Manthan Patel
Proofreader: Safis Editing
Indexer: Pratik Shirodkar
Graphics: Tania Dutta
Production Coordinator: Deepika Naik

First published: March 2018

Production reference: 1070318

Published by Packt Publishing Ltd.
Livery Place
35 Livery Street
Birmingham
B3 2PB, UK.

ISBN 978-1-78883-799-6

www.packtpub.com

To my wife, Lana, whose love and support define the best epoch of my life

To my son, William, who is likely disappointed that this book doesn't have more dragons in it

To my mother, Sharon, and to the memory of my father, Bob, who taught me that determination and resilience matter more than intelligence

`mapt.io`

Mapt is an online digital library that gives you full access to over 5,000 books and videos, as well as industry leading tools to help you plan your personal development and advance your career. For more information, please visit our website.

Why subscribe?

- Spend less time learning and more time coding with practical eBooks and Videos from over 4,000 industry professionals

- Improve your learning with Skill Plans built especially for you

- Get a free eBook or video every month

- Mapt is fully searchable

- Copy and paste, print, and bookmark content

PacktPub.com

Did you know that Packt offers eBook versions of every book published, with PDF and ePub files available? You can upgrade to the eBook version at `www.PacktPub.com` and as a print book customer, you are entitled to a discount on the eBook copy. Get in touch with us at `service@packtpub.com` for more details.

At `www.PacktPub.com`, you can also read a collection of free technical articles, sign up for a range of free newsletters, and receive exclusive discounts and offers on Packt books and eBooks.

Foreword

I first met Mike Bernico when we were two of the founding members of a new data science team at a Fortune 50 company. Then, it was a heady time; there wasn't such a thing as formal data science education, so we were all self-taught. We were a collection of adventurous people from diverse backgrounds, who identified and learned data science techniques because we needed them to solve the problems that we were interested in. We built a team with an optimistic hacker approach—the belief that we could find and apply techniques "from the wild" to build interesting, useful things.

It is in this practical, scrappy spirit that Mike wrote *Deep Learning Quick Reference* book. Deep learning is frequently made out to be mysterious and difficult; however, in this guide, Mike breaks down major deep learning techniques, making them approachable and applicable. With this book, you (yes, you!) can quickly get started with using deep learning for your own projects in a variety of different modalities.

Mike has been practising data science since before the discipline was named, and he has been specifically teaching the topic to university students for 3 years. Prior to this, he spent many years as a working computer scientist with a specialization in networks and security, and he also has a knack for engaging with people and communicating with nonspecialists. He is currently the Lead Data Scientist for a large financial services company, where he designs systems for data science, builds machine learning models with direct applications and for research publications, mentors junior data scientists, and teaches stakeholders about data science. He knows his stuff!

With *Deep Learning Quick Reference* book, you'll benefit from Mike's deep experience, humor, and down-to-earth manner as you build example networks alongside him. After you complete Mike's book, you'll have the confidence and knowledge to understand and apply deep learning to the problems of your own devising, for both fun and function.

Bon voyage, and good hacking!

- J. Malia Andrus, Ph.D.

Data Scientist
Seattle Washington

Contributors

About the author

Mike Bernico is a Lead Data Scientist at State Farm Mutual Insurance Companies. He also works as an adjunct for the University of Illinois at Springfield, where he teaches Essentials of Data Science, and Advanced Neural Networks and Deep Learning. Mike earned his MSCS from the University of Illinois at Springfield. He's an advocate for open source software and the good it can bring to the world. As a lifelong learner with umpteen hobbies, Mike also enjoys cycling, travel photography, and wine making.

I'd like to thank the very talented State Farm Data Scientists, current and past, for their friendship, expertise, and encouragement.
Thanks to my technical reviewers for providing insight and assistance with this book.
Most importantly, I'd like to thank my wife, Lana, and my son, Will, for making time for this in our lives.

About the reviewer

Vitor Bianchi Lanzetta has a master's degree in Applied Economics from the University of São Paulo, one of the most reputable universities in Latin America. He has done a lot of research in economics using neural networks. He has also authored *R Data Visualization Recipes*, Packt Publishing. Vitor is very passionate about data science in general, and he walks the earth with a personal belief that he is just as cool as he is geek. He thinks that you will learn a lot from this book, and that TensorFlow may be the greatest deep learning tool currently available.

Packt is searching for authors like you

If you're interested in becoming an author for Packt, please visit `authors.packtpub.com` and apply today. We have worked with thousands of developers and tech professionals, just like you, to help them share their insight with the global tech community. You can make a general application, apply for a specific hot topic that we are recruiting an author for, or submit your own idea.

Table of Contents

Preface

Deep Learning Quick Reference demonstrates a fast and practical approach to using deep learning. It's focused on real-life problems, and it provides just enough theory and math to reinforce the readers' understanding of the topic. Deep learning is an exciting, fast paced branch of machine learning, but it's also a field that can be broken into. It's a field where a flood of detailed, complicated research is created every day, and this can be overwhelming. In this book, I focus on teaching you the skills to apply deep learning on a variety of practical problems. My greatest hope for this book is that it will provide you with the tools you need to use deep learning techniques to solve your machine learning problems.

Who this book is for

I'm a practicing data scientist, and I'm writing this book keeping other practicing data scientists and machine learning engineers in mind. If you're a software engineer applying deep learning, this book is also for you.

If you're a deep learning researcher, then this book isn't really for you; however, you should still pick up a copy so that you can criticize the lack of proofs and mathematical rigor in this book.

If you're an academic or educator, then this book is definitely for you. I've taught a survey source in data science at the University of Illinois at Springfield (go Prairie Stars!) for the past 3 years, and in doing so, I've had the opportunity to inspire a number of future machine learning people. This experience has inspired me to create this book. I think a book like this is a great way to help students build interest in a very complex topic.

What this book covers

Chapter 1, *The Building Blocks of Deep Learning*, reviews some basics around the operation of neural networks, touches on optimization algorithms, talks about model validation, and goes over setting up a development environment suitable for building deep neural networks.

Chapter 2, *Using Deep Learning to Solve Regression Problems*, enables you build very simple neural networks to solve regression problems and explore the impact of deeper more complex models on those problems.

Chapter 3, *Monitoring Network Training Using TensorBoard*, lets you get started right away with TensorBoard, which is a wonderful application for monitoring and debugging your future models.

Chapter 4, *Using Deep Learning to Solve Binary Classification Problems*, helps you solve binary classification problems using deep learning.

Chapter 5, *Using Keras to Solve Multiclass Classification Problems*, takes you to multiclass classification and explores the differences. It also talks about managing overfitting and the safest choices for doing so.

Chapter 6, *Hyperparameter Optimization*, shows two separate methods for model tuning—one, well-known and battle tested, while the other is a state-of-the-art method.

Chapter 7, *Training a CNN From Scratch*, teaches you how to use convolutional networks to do classification with images.

Chapter 8, *Transfer Learning with Pretrained CNNs*, describes how to apply transfer learning to get amazing performance from an image classifier, even with very little data.

Chapter 9, *Training an RNN from scratch*, discusses RNNs and LSTMS, and how to use them for time series forecasting problems.

Chapter 10, *Training LSTMs with Word Embeddings From Scratch*, continues our conversation on LSTMs, this time talking about natural language classification tasks.

Chapter 11, *Training Seq2Seq Models*, helps us use sequence to sequence models to do machine translation.

Chapter 12, *Using Deep Reinforcement Learning*, introduces deep reinforcement learning and builds a deep Q network that can power autonomous agents.

Chapter 13, *Generative Adversarial Networks*, explains how to use generative adversarial networks to generate convincing images.

To get the most out of this book

1. I assume that you're already experienced with more traditional data science and predictive modeling techniques such as Linear/Logistic Regression and Random Forest. If this is your first experience with machine learning, this may be a little difficult for you.
2. I also assume that you have at least some experience in programming with Python, or at least another programming language such as Java or C++.
3. Deep learning is computationally intensive, and some of the models we build here require an NVIDIA GPU to run in a reasonable amount of time. If you don't own a fast GPU, you may wish to use a GPU-based cloud instance on either Amazon Web Services or Google Cloud Platform.

Download the example code files

You can download the example code files for this book from your account at `www.packtpub.com`. If you purchased this book elsewhere, you can visit `www.packtpub.com/support` and register to have the files emailed directly to you.

You can download the code files by following these steps:

1. Log in or register at `www.packtpub.com`.
2. Select the **SUPPORT** tab.
3. Click on **Code Downloads & Errata**.
4. Enter the name of the book in the **Search** box and follow the onscreen instructions.

Once the file is downloaded, make sure that you unzip or extract the folder using the latest version of any of these:

*   WinRAR/7-Zip for Windows
*   Zipeg/iZip/UnRarX for macOS
*   7-Zip/PeaZip for Linux

The code bundle for the book is also hosted on GitHub at
`https://github.com/PacktPublishing/Deep-Learning-Quick-Reference`. We also have
other code bundles from our rich catalog of books and videos available at `https://github.com/PacktPublishing/`. Check them out!

Conventions used

There are a number of text conventions used throughout this book.

`CodeInText`: Indicates code words in text, database table names, folder names, filenames,
file extensions, pathnames, dummy URLs, user input, and Twitter handles. Here is an
example: "That's exactly what the `ModelCheckpoint` callback does for us."

A block of code is set as follows:

```
def binary_accuracy(y_true, y_pred):
    return K.mean(K.equal(y_true, K.round(y_pred)), axis=-1)
```

When we wish to draw your attention to a particular part of a code block, the relevant lines
or items are set in bold:

```
def build_network(input_features=None):
    inputs = Input(shape=(input_features,), name="input")
    x = Dense(32, activation='relu', name="hidden1")(inputs)
    x = Dense(32, activation='relu', name="hidden2")(x)
    x = Dense(32, activation='relu', name="hidden3")(x)
    x = Dense(32, activation='relu', name="hidden4")(x)
    x = Dense(16, activation='relu', name="hidden5")(x)
    prediction = Dense(1, activation='linear', name="final")(x)
    model = Model(inputs=inputs, outputs=prediction)
    model.compile(optimizer='adam', loss='mean_absolute_error')
    return model
```

Any command-line input or output is written as follows:

```
model-weights.00-0.971304.hdf5
model-weights.02-0.977391.hdf5
model-weights.05-0.985217.hdf5
```

Bold: Indicates a new term, an important word, or words that you see onscreen. For
example, words in menus or dialog boxes appear in the text like this. Here is an example:
"Select **System info** from the **Administration** panel."

Warnings or important notes appear like this.

 Tips and tricks appear like this.

Get in touch

Feedback from our readers is always welcome.

General feedback: Email feedback@packtpub.com and mention the book title in the subject of your message. If you have questions about any aspect of this book, please email us at questions@packtpub.com.

Errata: Although we have taken every care to ensure the accuracy of our content, mistakes do happen. If you have found a mistake in this book, we would be grateful if you would report this to us. Visit www.packtpub.com/submit-errata, select your book, click on the Errata Submission Form link, and enter the details.

Piracy: If you come across any illegal copies of our works in any form on the internet, we would be grateful if you would provide us with the location address or website name. Please contact us at copyright@packtpub.com with a link to the material.

If you are interested in becoming an author: If there is a topic that you have expertise in and you are interested in either writing or contributing to a book, please visit authors.packtpub.com.

Reviews

Please leave a review. Once you have read and used this book, why not leave a review on the site that you purchased it from? Potential readers can then see and use your unbiased opinion to make purchase decisions; also, we at Packt can understand what you think about our products, and our authors can see your feedback on their book. Thank you!

For more information about Packt, please visit packtpub.com.

1
The Building Blocks of Deep Learning

Welcome to *Deep Learning Quick Reference*! In this book, I am going to attempt to make deep learning techniques more accessible, practical, and consumable to data scientists, machine learning engineers, and software engineers who need to solve problems with deep learning. If you want to train your own deep neural network and you're stuck somewhere, there is a good chance this guide will help.

This book is hands on and is intended to be a practical guide that can help you solve your problems fast. It is primarily intended for experienced machine learning engineers and data scientists who need to use deep learning to solve a problem. Aside from this chapter, which provides some of the terminology, frameworks, and background that we will need to get started, it's not meant to be read in order. Each chapter contains a practical example, complete with code and a few best practices and safe choices. We expect you to flip to the chapter you need and get started.

This book won't go deeply into the theory of deep learning and neural networks. There are many wonderful books that can provide that background, and I highly recommend that you read at least one of them (maybe a bibliography or just recommendations). We hope to provide just enough theory and mathematical intuition to get you started.

We will cover the following topics in this chapter:

- Deep neural network architectures
- Optimization algorithms for deep learning
- Deep learning frameworks
- Building datasets for deep learning

The deep neural network architectures

The deep neural network architectures can vary greatly in structure depending on the network's application, but they all have some basic components. In this section, we will talk briefly about those components.

In this book, I'll define a deep neural network as a network with more than a single hidden layer. Beyond that we won't attempt to limit the membership to the *Deep Learning Club*. As such, our networks might have less than 100 neurons, or possibly millions. We might use special layers of neurons, including convolutions and recurrent layers, but we will refer to all of these as neurons nonetheless.

Neurons

A neuron is the atomic unit of a neural network. This is sometimes inspired by biology; however, that's a topic for a different book. Neurons are typically arranged into layers. In this book, if I'm referring to a specific neuron, I'll use the notation n_k^l where l is the layer the neuron is in and k is the neuron number. As we will be using programming languages that observe 0th notation, my notation will also be 0th based.

At their core, most neurons are composed of two functions that work together: a linear function and an activation function. Let us take a high-level look at those two components.

The neuron linear function

The first component of the neuron is a linear function whose output is the sum of the inputs, each multiplied by a coefficient. This function is really more or less a linear regression. These coefficients are typically referred to as weights in neural network speak. For example, given some neuron with the input features of *x1*, *x2*, and *x3*, and output *z*, this linear component or the neuron linear function would simply be:

$$z = x_1\theta_1 + x_2\theta_2 + x_3\theta_3 + b$$

Where $\{\theta_1, \theta_2, \ldots \theta_n\}$ are weights or coefficients that we will need to learn given the data and b is a bias term.

Neuron activation functions

The second function of the neuron is the activation function, which is tasked with introducing a nonlinearity between neurons. A commonly used activation is the sigmoid activation, which you may be familiar with from logistic regression. It squeezes the output of the neuron into an output space where very large values of z are driven to 1 and very small values of z are driven to 0.

The sigmoid function looks like this:

$$sigmoid(z) = \frac{1}{1 + e^{-z}}$$

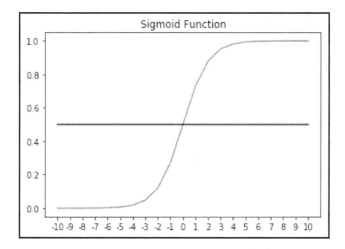

It turns out that the activation function is very important for intermediate neurons. Without it one could prove that a stack of neurons with linear activation's (which is really no activation, or more formally an activation function where z=z) is really just a single linear function.

A single linear function is undesirable in this case because there are many scenarios where our network may be under specified for the problem at hand. That is to say that the network can't model the data well because of non-linear relationships present in the data between the input features and target variable (what we're predicting).

The canonical example of a function that cannot be modeled with a linear function is the exclusive OR function, which is shown in the following figure:

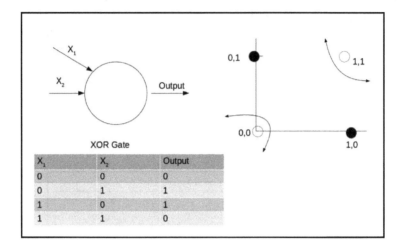

Other common activation functions are the tanh function and the ReLu or Rectilinear Activation.

The hyperbolic tangent or the tanh function looks like this:

$$tanh(z) = \frac{e^z - e^{-z}}{e^z + e^{-z}}$$

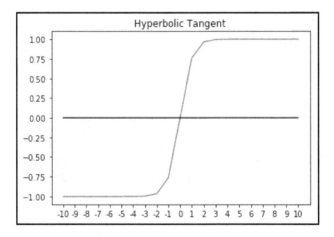

The `tanh` usually works better than sigmoid for intermediate layers. As you can probably see, the output of `tanh` will be between [-1, 1], whereas the output of sigmoid is [0, 1]. This additional width provides some resilience from a phenomenon known as the vanishing/exploding gradient problem, which we will cover in more detail later. For now, it's enough to know that the vanishing gradient problem can cause networks to converge very slowly in the early layers, if at all. Because of that, networks using `tanh` will tend to converge somewhat faster than networks that use sigmoid activation. That said, they are still not as fast as ReLu.

ReLu, or Rectilinear Activation, is defined simply as:

$$f(z) = max(0, z)$$

It's a safe bet and we will use it most of the time throughout this book. Not only is ReLu easy to compute and differentiate, it's also resilient against the vanishing gradient problem. The only drawback to ReLu is that it's first derivative is undefined at exactly 0. Variants including leaky ReLu, are computationally harder, but more robust against this issue.

For completeness, here's a somewhat obvious graph of ReLu:

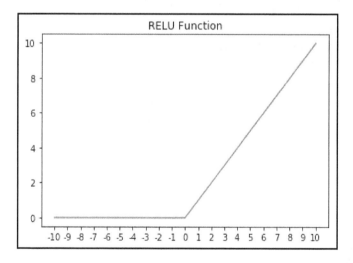

The loss and cost functions in deep learning

Every machine learning model really starts with a cost function. Simply, a cost function allows you to measure how well your model is fitting the training data. In this book, we will define the loss function as the correctness of fit for a single observation within the training set. The cost function will then most often be an average of the loss across the training set. We will revisit loss functions later when we introduce each type of neural network; however, quickly consider the cost function for linear regression as an example:

$$J = \frac{1}{2m} \sum_{i=1}^{m} (\hat{y} - y)^2$$

In this case, the loss function would be $(\hat{y} - y)^2$, which is really the squared error. So then J, our `cost` function, is really just the mean squared error, or an average of the squared error across the entire dataset. The term 1/2 is added to make some of the calculus cleaner by convention.

The forward propagation process

Forward propagation is the process by which we attempt to predict our target variable using the features present in a single observation. Imagine we had a two-layer neural network. In the forward propagation process, we would start with the features present within that observation $\{x_1, x_2, \ldots x_n\}$ and then multiply those features by their associated coefficients within layer 1 and add a bias term for each neuron. After that, we would send that output to the activation for the neuron. Following that, the output would be sent to the next layer, and so on, until we reach the end of the network where we are left with our network's prediction:

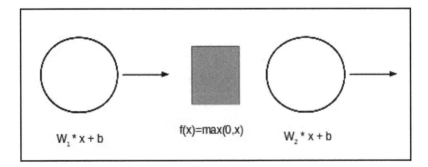

The back propagation function

Once forward propagation is complete, we have the network's prediction for each data point. We also know that data point's actual value. Typically, the prediction is defined as $\hat{y}$ while the actual value of the target variable is defined as y.

Once both y and $\hat{y}$ are known, the network's error can be computed using the cost function. Recall that the cost function is the average of the `loss` function.

In order for learning to occur within the network, the network's error signal must be propagated backwards through the network layers from the last layer to the first. Our goal in back propagation is to propagate this error signal backwards through the network while using it to update the network weights as the signal travels. Mathematically, to do so we need to minimize the cost function by nudging the weights towards values that make the cost function the smallest. This process is called gradient descent.

The gradient is the partial derivative of the error function with respect to each weight within the network. The gradient of each weight can be calculated, layer by layer, using the chain rule and the gradients of the layers above.

Once the gradients of each layer are known, we can use the gradient descent algorithm to minimize the `cost` function.

The Gradient Descent will repeat this update until the network's error is minimized and the process has converged:

$$\theta = \theta - \alpha \frac{\partial J}{\partial \theta}$$

The gradient descent algorithm multiples the gradient by a learning rate called **alpha** and subtracts that value from the current value of each weight. The learning rate is a hyperparameter.

Stochastic and minibatch gradient descents

The algorithm describe in the previous section assumes a forward and corresponding backwards pass over the entire dataset and as such it's called batch gradient descent.

Another possible way to do gradient descent would be to use a single data point at a time, updating the network weights as we go. This method might help speed up convergence around saddle points where the network might stop converging. Of course, the error estimation of only a single point may not be a very good approximation of the error of the entire dataset.

The best solution to this problem is using mini batch gradient descent, in which we will take some random subset of the data called a mini batch to compute our error and update our network weights. This is almost always the best option. It has the additional benefit of naturally splitting a very large dataset into chunks that are more easily managed in the memory of a machine, or even across machines.

 This is an extremely high-level description of one of the most important parts of a neural network, which we believe fits with the practical nature of this book. In practice, most modern frameworks handle these steps for us; however, they are most certainly worth knowing at least theoretically. We encourage the reader to go deeper into forward and backward propagation as time permits.

Optimization algorithms for deep learning

The gradient descent algorithm is not the only optimization algorithm available to optimize our network weights, however it's the basis for most other algorithms. While understanding every optimization algorithm out there is likely a PhD worth of material, we will devote a few sentences to some of the most practical.

Using momentum with gradient descent

Using gradient descent with momentum speeds up gradient descent by increasing the speed of learning in directions the gradient has been constant in direction while slowing learning in directions the gradient fluctuates in direction. It allows the velocity of gradient descent to increase.

Momentum works by introducing a velocity term, and using a weighted moving average of that term in the update rule, as follows:

$$v_t = \beta v_{t-1} + (1 - \beta)grad^2$$

$$\theta = \theta - v_t$$

Most typically β is set to 0.9 in the case of momentum, and usually this is not a hyper-parameter that needs to be changed.

The RMSProp algorithm

RMSProp is another algorithm that can speed up gradient descent by speeding up learning in some directions, and dampening oscillations in other directions, across the multidimensional space that the network weights represent:

$$grad = \frac{\partial J}{\partial \theta}$$

$$v_t = \beta v_{t-1} + (1 - \beta)grad^2$$

$$\theta = \theta - \alpha\frac{grad}{\sqrt{v_t}}$$

This has the effect of reducing oscillations more in directions where v_t is large.

The Adam optimizer

Adam is one of the best performing known **optimizer** and it's my first choice. It works well across a wide variety of problems. It combines the best parts of both momentum and RMSProp into a single update rule:

$$grad = \frac{\partial J}{\partial \theta}$$

$$m_t = \beta_1 m_{t-1} + (1 - \beta_1)grad$$

$$v_t = \beta_2 v_{t-1} + (1 - \beta_2)grad$$

$$\theta = \theta - \alpha\frac{m_t}{\sqrt{v_t + \epsilon}}$$

Where ϵ is some very small number to prevent division by 0.

 Adam is often a great choice, and it's a great place to start when you're prototyping, so save yourself some time by starting with Adam.

Deep learning frameworks

While it's most certainly possible to build and train deep neural networks from scratch using just Python's `numpy`, that would take a great deal of time and code. It's far more practical, in almost every case, to use a deep learning framework.

Throughout this book we will be using **TensorFlow** and **Keras** to make developing deep neural networks much easier and faster.

What is TensorFlow?

TensorFlow is a library that can be used to quickly build deep neural networks. In TensorFlow, the mathematical operations that we've covered thus far are expressed as nodes. The edges between these nodes are tensors, or multidimensional data arrays. TensorFlow can, given a neural network defined as a graph and a loss function, automatically compute gradients for the network and optimize the graph to minimize the loss function.

TensorFlow was released as an open source project by Google in 2015. Since then it has gained a very large following and enjoys a large user community. While TensorFlow provides APIs in Java, C++, Go, and Python, we will only be covering the Python API. The Python API is used in this book because it's both the most commonly used, and the API most commonly used for the development of new models.

TensorFlow can greatly accelerate computation by performing those calculations on one or more Graphics Processing Units. The acceleration that GPU computation provides has become a necessity in modern deep learning.

What is Keras?

While building deep neural networks in TensorFlow is far easier than doing it from scratch, TensorFlow is still a very low-level API. Keras is a high-level API that allows us to use TensorFlow (or alternatively Theano or Microsoft's CNTK) to rapidly build deep learning networks.

Models built in Keras and TensorFlow are portable and can be trained or served in native TensorFlow as well. Models constructed in TensorFlow can be loaded into Keras and used there as well.

Popular alternatives to TensorFlow

There are many other great deep learning frameworks out there. We chose Keras and TensorFlow primarily because of popularity, ease of use, availability for support, and readiness for production deployments. There are undoubtedly other worthy alternatives.

Some of my favorites alternatives to TensorFlow include:

- **Apache MXNet**: A very high performance framework with a great new imperative interface called **Gluon** (https://mxnet.apache.org/)
- **PyTorch**: A very new and promising architecture originally developed by Facebook (http://pytorch.org/)
- **CNTK:** Microsoft's deep learning framework that can also be used with Keras (https://www.microsoft.com/en-us/cognitive-toolkit/)

While I do strongly believe that Keras and TensorFlow are the correct choices for this book, I also want to acknowledge these great frameworks and the contributions to the field that each project has made.

GPU requirements for TensorFlow and Keras

For the remainder of the book, we will be using Keras and TensorFlow. Most of the examples we will be exploring require a GPU for acceleration. Most modern deep learning frameworks, including TensorFlow, use GPUs to greatly accelerate the vast amount of calculations required during network training. Without a GPU, the training time of most of the models we discuss will be unreasonably long.

If you don't have a computer with a GPU installed, GPU-based compute instances can be rented by the second from a variety of cloud providers including Amazon's Amazon Web Services and Google's Google Cloud Platform. For the examples in this book, we will be using a `p2.xlarge` instance in Amazon EC2 running Ubuntu Server 16.04. The p2.xlarge instance provides an Nvidia Tesla K80 GPU with 2,496 CUDA cores, which will make running the models we show in this book much faster than what is achievable on even very high end desktop computers.

Installing Nvidia CUDA Toolkit and cuDNN

Since you'll likely be using a cloud based solution for your deep learning work, I've included instructions that will get you up and running fast on Ubuntu Linux, which is commonly available across cloud providers. It's also possible to install TensorFlow and Keras on Windows. As of TensorFlow v1.2, TensorFlow unfortunately does not support GPUs on OS X.

Before we can utilize the GPU, the **NVidia CUDA Toolkit** and **cuDNN** must be installed. We will be installing CUDA Toolkit 8.0 and cuDNN v6.0, which are recommended for use with TensorFlow v1.4. There is a good chance that a new version will be released before you finish reading this paragraph, so check `www.tensorflow.org` for the latest required versions.

We will start by installing the `build-essential` package on Ubuntu, which contains most of what we need to compile C++ programs. The code is given here:

```
sudo apt-get update
sudo apt-get install build-essential
```

Next, we can download and install CUDA Toolkit. As previously mentioned, we will be installing version 8.0 and it's associated patch. You can find the CUDA Toolkit that is right for you at `https://developer.nvidia.com/cuda-zone`.

```
wget
https://developer.nvidia.com/compute/cuda/8.0/Prod2/local_installers/cuda_8
.0.61_375.26_linux-run
sudo sh cuda_8.0.61_375.26_linux-run # Accept the EULA and choose defaults
wget
https://developer.nvidia.com/compute/cuda/8.0/Prod2/patches/2/cuda_8.0.61.2
_linux-run
sudo sh cuda_8.0.61.2_linux-run # Accept the EULA and choose defaults
```

The CUDA Toolkit should now be installed in the following path: `/usr/local/cuda`. You'll need to add a few environment variables so that TensorFlow can find it. You should probably consider adding these environment variables to `~/.bash_profile`, so that they're set at every login, as shown in the following code:

```
export LD_LIBRARY_PATH="$LD_LIBRARY_PATH:/usr/local/cuda/lib64"
export CUDA_HOME="/usr/local/cuda"
```

At this point, you can test that everything is working by executing the following command: `nvidia-smi`. The output should look similar to this:

```
$nvidia-smi
+-----------------------------------------------------------------------------
---+
| NVIDIA-SMI 375.26 Driver Version: 375.26 |
|-------------------------------+----------------------+--------------------
----+
| GPU Name Persistence-M| Bus-Id Disp.A | Volatile Uncorr. ECC |
| Fan Temp Perf Pwr:Usage/Cap| Memory-Usage | GPU-Util Compute M. |
|===============================+======================+====================
===|
| 0 Tesla K80 Off | 0000:00:1E.0 Off | 0 |
| N/A 41C P0 57W / 149W | 0MiB / 11439MiB | 99% Default |
+-------------------------------+----------------------+--------------------
----+
```

Lastly, we need to install cuDNN, which is the NVIDIA CUDA Deep Neural Network library.

First, download cuDNN to your local computer. To do so, you will need to register as a developer in the **NVIDIA Developer Network**. You can find cuDNN at the cuDNN homepage at `https://developer.nvidia.com/cuDNN`. Once you have downloaded it to your local computer, you can use `scp` to move it to your EC2 instance. While exact instructions will vary by cloud provider you can find additional information about connecting to AWS EC2 via SSH/SCP at `https://docs.aws.amazon.com/AWSEC2/latest/UserGuide/AccessingInstancesLinux.html`.

Once you've moved cuDNN to your EC2 image, you can unpack the file, using the following code:

```
tar -xzvf cudnn-8.0-linux-x64-v6.0.tgz
```

Finally, copy the unpacked files to their appropriate locations, using the following code:

```
sudo cp cuda/include/cudnn.h /usr/local/cuda/include/
sudo cp cuda/lib64/* /usr/local/cuda/lib64
```

It's unclear to me why CUDA and cuDNN are distributed separately and why cuDNN requires registrations. The overly complicated download process and manual installation of cuDNN is really one of the greatest mysteries in deep learning.

Installing Python

We will be using `virtualenv` to create an isolated Python virtual environment. While this isn't strictly necessary, it's an excellent practice. By doing so, we will keep all our Python libraries for this project in a separate isolated environment that won't interfere with the system Python installation. Additionally, `virtualenv` environments will make it easier to package and deploy our deep neural networks later on.

Let's start by installing `Python`, `pip`, and `virtualenv`, using the aptitude package manager in Ubuntu. The following is the code:

```
sudo apt-get install python3-pip python3-dev python-virtualenv
```

Now we can create a virtual environment for our work. We will be keeping all our virtual environment files in a folder called `~/deep-learn`. You are free to choose any name you wish for this virtual environment. The following code shows how to create a virtual environment:

```
virtualenv --no-site-packages -p python3 ~/deep-learn
```

If you're an experienced Python developer, you might have noticed that I've set up the environment to default to Python 3.x. That's most certainly not required, and TensorFlow / Keras both support Python 2.7. That said, the author feels a moral obligation to the Python community to support modern versions of Python.

Now that the virtual environment has been created, you can activate it as follows:

```
$source ~/deep-learn/bin/activate
(deep-learn)$ # notice the shell changes to indicate the virtualenv
```

At this point, every time you log in you will need to activate the virtual environment you want to work in. If you would like to always enter the virtual environment you just created, you can add the source command to `~/.bash_profile`.

Now that we've configured our virtual environment, we can add Python packages as required within it. To start, let's make sure we have the latest version of `pip`, the Python package manager:

```
easy_install -U pip
```

Lastly, I recommend installing IPython, which is an interactive Python shell that makes development much easier.

```
pip install ipython
```

And that's it. Now we're ready to install TensorFlow and Keras.

Installing TensorFlow and Keras

After everything we've just been through together, you'll be pleased to see how straightforward installing TensorFlow and Keras now is.

Let's start with installing TensorFlow

The installation of TensorFlow can be done using the following code:

```
pip install --upgrade tensorflow-gpu
```

Be sure to pip install `tensorflow-gpu`. If you pip install TensorfFow (without `-gpu`), you will install the CPU-only version.

Before we install Keras, let's test our TensorFlow installation. To do this, I'll be using some sample code from the TensorfFow website and the IPython interpreter.

Start the **IPython** interpreter by typing **IPython** at the bash prompt. Once **IPython** has started, let's attempt to import TensorFlow. The output would look like the following:

```
In [1]: import tensorflow as tf
In [2]:
```

If importing TensorFlow results in an error, troubleshoot the steps you have followed so far. Most often when TensorFlow cannot be imported, the CUDA or cuDNN might not be installed correctly.

Now that we've successfully installed TensorFlow, we will run a tiny bit of code in IPython that will verify we can run computations on the GPU:

```
a = tf.constant([1.0,</span> 2.0, 3.0, 4.0, 5.0, 6.0], shape=[2, 3],
name='a')
b = tf.constant([1.0, 2.0, 3.0, 4.0, 5.0, 6.0], shape=[3, 2], name='b')
c = tf.matmul(a, b)
sess = tf.Session(config=tf.ConfigProto(log_device_placement=True))
print(sess.run(c))
```

If everything goes as we hope, we will see lots of indications that our GPU is being used. I have included some output here and highlighted the evidence to draw your attention to it. Your output will likely be different based on hardware, but you should see similar evidence the one shown here:

```
/job:localhost/replica:0/task:0/device:GPU:0 -> device: 0, name: Tesla K80,
pci bus id: 0000:00:1e.0, compute capability: 3.7
MatMul: (MatMul): /job:localhost/replica:0/task:0/device:GPU:0
: I tensorflow/core/common_runtime/placer.cc:874] MatMul:
(MatMul)/job:localhost/replica:0/task:0/device:GPU:0
 b: (Const): /job:localhost/replica:0/task:0/device:GPU:0
: I tensorflow/core/common_runtime/placer.cc:874] b:
(Const)/job:localhost/replica:0/task:0/device:GPU:0
 a: (Const): /job:localhost/replica:0/task:0/device:GPU:0
: I tensorflow/core/common_runtime/placer.cc:874] a:
(Const)/job:localhost/replica:0/task:0/device:GPU:0
 [[ 22. 28.]
 [ 49. 64.]]
```

In the preceding output, we can see that tensors a and b, as well as the matrix multiplication operation, were assigned the the GPU. If there was a problem with accessing the GPU, the output might look as follows:

```
I tensorflow/core/common_runtime/placer.cc:874] b_1:
(Const)/job:localhost/replica:0/task:0/device:CPU:0
a_1: (Const): /job:localhost/replica:0/task:0/device:CPU:0
I tensorflow/core/common_runtime/placer.cc:874] a_1:
(Const)/job:localhost/replica:0/task:0/device:CPU:0
```

Here we can see the tensors b_1 and a_1 were assigned to the CPU rather than the GPU. If this happens there is a problem with your installation of TensorFlow, CUDA, or cuDNN.

If you've made it this far, you have a working installation of TensorFlow. The only remaining task is to install Keras.

The installation of Keras can be done with the help of the following code:

```
pip install keras
```

And that's it! Now we're ready to build deep neural networks in Keras and TensorFlow.

 This might be a great time to create a snapshot or even an AMI of your EC2 instance, so that you don't have to go through this installation again.

Building datasets for deep learning

Compared to other predictive models that you might have used, deep neural networks are very complicated. Consider a network with 100 inputs, two hidden layers with 30 neurons each, and a logistic output layer. That network would have 3,930 learnable parameters as well as the hyperparameters needed for optimization, and that's a very small example. A large convolutional neural network will have hundreds of millions of learnable parameters. All these parameters are what make deep neural networks so amazing at learning structures and patterns. However, this also makes overfitting possible.

Bias and variance errors in deep learning

You may be familiar with the so-called bias/variance trade-off in typical predictive models. In case you're not, we'll provide a quick reminder here. With traditional predictive models, there is usually some compromise when we try to find an error from bias and an error from variance. So let's see what these two errors are:

- **Bias error**: Bias error is the error that is introduced by the model. For example, if you attempted to model a non-linear function with a linear model, your model would be *under specified* and the bias error would be high.
- **Variance error**: Variance error is the error that is introduced by randomness in the training data. When we fit our training distribution so well that our model no longer generalizes, we have overfit or introduce a variance error.

In most machine learning applications, we seek to find some compromise that minimizes bias error, while introducing as little variance error as possible. I say most because one of the great things about deep neural networks is that, for the most part, bias and variance can be manipulated independently of one another. However, to do so, we will need to be very careful with how we structure our training data.

The train, val, and test datasets

For the rest of the book, I will be structuring my data into three separate sets that I'll refer to as train, val, and test. These three separate datasets, drawn as random samples from the total dataset will be structured and sized approximately like this.

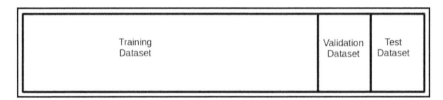

The train dataset will be used for training the network, as expected.

The val dataset, or the validation dataset, will be used to find ideal hyperparameters, and to measure overfitting. At the end of an *epoch,* which is when the network has has the opportunity to observe every data point in the training set, we will make a prediction on the val set. That prediction will be used to watch for overfitting and will help us know when the network has finished training. Using the val set at the end of each epoch like this somewhat differs from the typical usage. For more information on Hold-Out Validation please reference The Elements of Statistical Learning by Hastie and Tibshirani (`https://web.stanford.edu/~hastie/ElemStatLearn/`).

The test dataset will be used once all training is complete, to accurately measure model performance on a set of data that the network hasn't seen.

It is very important that the val and test data comes from the same datasets. It is less important that the train dataset matches val and test, although that is still ideal. If image augmentation were being used (performing minor modifications to training images in an attempt to amplify the training set size) for example, the training set distribution may no longer match the val set distribution. This is acceptable and network performance can be adequately measured as long as val and test are from the same distribution.

In traditional machine learning applications it's somewhat customary to use 10-20 percent of the available data for val and test. In deep neural networks it's often the case that our data volume is so large that we can adequately measure network performance with much smaller val and test sets. When data volume goes into the 10s of millions of observations, a 98 percent, 1 percent, 1 percent split may be completely appropriate.

Managing bias and variance in deep neural networks

Now that we've defined how we will structure data and refreshed ourselves on bias and variance, let's consider how we will control bias and variance errors in our deep neural networks.

- **High bias**: A network with high bias will have a very high error rate when predicting on the training set. The model is not doing well at fitting the data. In order to reduce the bias you will likely need to change the network architecture. You may need to add layers, neurons, or both. It may be that your problem is better solved using a convolutional or recurrent network.

  Of course, sometimes a problem is high bias because of a lack of signal or very difficult problem, so be sure to calibrate your expectations on a reasonable rate (I like to start by calibrating on human accuracy).

- **High variance**: A network with a low bias error is fitting the training data well; however, if the validation error is greater than the test error the network has begun to overfit the training data. The two best ways to reduce variance are by adding data and adding regularization to the network.

  Adding data is straightforward but not always possible. Throughout the book, we will cover regularization techniques as they apply. The most common regularization techniques we will talk about are L2 regularization, dropout, and batch normalization.

K-Fold cross-validation

If you're experienced with machine learning, you may be wondering why I would opt for Hold-Out (train/val/test) validation over K-Fold cross-validation. Training a deep neural network is a very expensive operation, and put very simply, training K of them per set of hyperparameters we'd like to explore is usually not very practical.

We can be somewhat confident that Hold-Out validation does a very good job, given a large enough val and test set. Most of the time, we are hopefully applying deep learning in situations where we have an abundance of data, resulting in an adequate val and test set.

Ultimately, it's up to you. As we will see later, Keras provides a **scikit-learn** interface that allows Keras models to be integrated into a scikit-learn pipeline. This allows us to perform K-Fold, Stratified K-Fold, and even grid searches with K-Fold. It's both possible and appropriate to sometimes use K-Fold CV in training deep models. That said, for the rest of the book we will focus on the using Hold-Out validation.

Summary

Hopefully, this chapter served to refresh your memory on deep neural network architectures and optimization algorithms. Because this is a quick reference we didn't go into much detail and I'd encourage the reader to dig deeper into any material here that might be new or unfamiliar.

We talked about the basics of Keras and TensorFlow and why we chose those frameworks for this book. We also talked about the installation and configuration of CUDA, cuDNN, Keras, and TensorFlow.

Lastly, we covered the Hold-Out validation methodology we will use throughout the remainder of the book and why we prefer it to K-Fold CV for most deep neural network applications.

We will be referring back to this chapter quite a bit as we revisit these topics in the chapters to come. In the next chapter, we will start using Keras to solve regression problems, as a first step into building deep neural networks.

2
Using Deep Learning to Solve Regression Problems

In this chapter, we will build a simple **multilayer perceptron** (**MLP**), which is a fancy name for a neural network with a single hidden layer, to solve a regression problem. Then we will go deeper with a deep neural network that has several hidden layers. Along the way, we will explore model performance and over fitting. So, let's get started!

We will cover the following topics in this chapter:

- Regression analysis and deep neural networks
- Using deep neural networks for regression
- Building an MLP in Keras
- Building a deep neural network in Keras
- Saving and loading a trained Keras model

Regression analysis and deep neural networks

In classic regression analysis, we use a linear model to learn the relationship between a set of independent variables and a dependent variable. In finding this relationship, we expect to be able to predict the value of the dependent variable given the values of the independent variables.

A second important reason to do regression analysis is to understand the impact a single independent variable has on the dependent variable when all other independent variables are held constant. One of the great things about traditional multiple linear regression is the *ceteris paribus* property of linear models. We can interpret the impact a single independent variable has on the dependent variable without consideration to the other independent variable by using the learned weight associated with that independent variable. This type of interpretation is challenging at best and requires us to make quite a few assumptions about our data and our model; however, it is often quite useful.

Deep neural networks aren't easily interpretable, although attempting to do so is an active field of study.

For an introduction to the current state of interpreting deep neural networks, check out Methods for Interpreting and Understanding Deep Neural Networks by Montavon and others (`https://arxiv.org/abs/1706.07979`).

Benefits of using a neural network for regression

For the rest of this chapter, we will focus on using deep neural networks to make a prediction. When compared to using traditional multiple linear regression, you'll be pleased to find that our neural network has the following advantages:

- We don't need to select or screen features. Neural networks are amazing feature engineering machines and can learn what features are relevant and ignore the irrelevant ones.
- Given an adequately complex network, feature interactions are also learned (for example, the effect of $x_1 * x_2$ in addition to the independent effects of x_1 and x_2)
- As you have maybe guessed by now, we can also learn higher order polynomial relationships (for example, x_2^3)
- And lastly, we don't have to constrain ourselves to only modelling normal distributions, or using different models for non-normal distributions, so long as we make sure our final activation can possibly model the distribution.

Drawbacks to consider when using a neural network for regression

But it's not all rainbows and kittens, there are some drawbacks to using a neural network for these really straightforward problems. The most notable drawbacks are:

- As previously noted, neural networks aren't easily interpretable.
- Neural Networks work best when there are many features and a lot of data. Many simple regression problems aren't large enough to really benefit from Neural Networks.
- Much of the time a traditional multiple regression, or a tree model such as Gradient Boosted Trees will outperform a neural network on problems such as this. The more complex, the better the fit for neural networks.

Using deep neural networks for regression

Now that you hopefully understand why you would (and would not) want to use deep neural networks for regression, I'll show you how to do it. While it's not quite as simple as using **linear regressor** in **scikit-learn**, I think you'll find it quite easy using **Keras**. Most importantly, Keras will allow you to quickly iterate through model architectures without changing a lot of code.

How to plan a machine learning problem

When building a new neural network, I recommend following the same basic steps every time.

Deep neural networks can get very complicated, very quickly. A little bit of planning and organization and greatly accelerate your workflow!

The following are the steps for building a deep neural network:

1. Outline the problem you're trying to solve.
2. Identify the inputs and outputs of the model.
3. Choose a `cost` function and metrics.
4. Create an initial network architecture.
5. Train and tune the network.

Defining our example problem

In our example problem, we will be using a wine quality dataset created by P. Cortez et al. (`https://archive.ics.uci.edu/ml/datasets/wine+quality`). We will be predicting the percentage of alcohol present in the white wine data, given the wine's 10 other chemical traits.

There are 4,898 total observations or elements in this dataset, which is perhaps large for a classic regression problem but it's quite small for a deep learning problem.

Some quick exploratory data analysis will tell us that the 10 chemical traits we'll be using to predict alcohol content are all continuous variables, on various scales.

Loading the dataset

While maybe not the most fun part of a machine learning problem, loading the data is an important step. I'm going to cover my data loading methodology here so that you can get a feel for how I handle loading a dataset.

```
from sklearn.preprocessing import StandardScaler
import pandas as pd

TRAIN_DATA = "./data/train/train_data.csv"
VAL_DATA = "./data/val/val_data.csv"
TEST_DATA = "./data/test/test_data.csv"

def load_data():
  """Loads train, val, and test datasets from disk"""
  train = pd.read_csv(TRAIN_DATA)
  val = pd.read_csv(VAL_DATA)
  test = pd.read_csv(TEST_DATA)

  # we will use sklearn's StandardScaler to scale our data to 0 mean, unit
```

```
variance.
 scaler = StandardScaler()
 train = scaler.fit_transform(train)
 val = scaler.transform(val)
 test = scaler.transform(test)
 # we will use a dict to keep all this data tidy.
 data = dict()

 data["train_y"] = train[:, 10]
 data["train_X"] = train[:, 0:9]
 data["val_y"] = val[:, 10]
 data["val_X"] = val[:, 0:9]
 data["test_y"] = test[:, 10]
 data["test_X"] = test[:, 0:9]
 # it's a good idea to keep the scaler (or at least the mean/variance) so
we can unscale predictions
 data["scaler"] = scaler
 return data
```

When I'm reading data from csv, excel, or even a DBMS, my first step is usually loading it into a pandas dataframe.

It's important to normalize our data so that each feature is on a comparable scale, and that all those scales fall within the bounds of our activation functions. Here, I used Scikit-Learn's `StandardScaler` to accomplish this task.

This gives us an overall dataset with shape (4898, 10). Our target variable, `alcohol`, is given as a percentage between 8% and 14.2%.

I've randomly sampled and divided the data into `train`, `val`, and `test` datasets prior to loading the data, so we don't have to worry about that here.

Lastly, the load_data() function returns a dictionary that keeps everything tidy and in one place. If you see me reference data["X_train"] later, just know that I'm referencing the training dataset, that I've stored in a dictionary of data.

. The code and data for this project are both available on the book's GitHub site (`https://github.com/mbernico/deep_learning_quick_reference`).

Defining our cost function

For regression tasks, the most common cost functions are **Root Mean Squared Error** (**RMSE**) and **Mean Absolute Error** (**MAE**). I'll be using MAE here. It is defined as follows:

$$MAE = \frac{1}{n} \sum_{j=1}^{n} |y_j - \hat{y}_j|$$

Very simply, MAE is the average unsigned error for all examples in the dataset. It's very similar to RMSE; however, we use the absolute value of the difference between y and $\hat{y}$ instead of the square root of the average squared error:

$$RMSE = \sqrt{\frac{1}{n} \sum_{j=1}^{n} (y_j - \hat{y}_j)^2}$$

You might be wondering how MAE differs from the more familiar RMSE. In cases where the error is evenly distributed across the dataset, RMSE and MAE will be equal. In cases where there are very large outliers in a dataset, RMSE will be much larger than MAE. Your choice of cost function should be appropriate to your use case. In regard to interpretability, MAE is more interpretable than RMSE as it's the actual average error.

Building an MLP in Keras

Keras uses an instance of a model object to contain a neural network. For those of you familiar with scikit-learn, this is probably quite familiar. What is somewhat different is that Keras models contain a set of layers. This set of layers needs to be defined by us. This allows for amazing flexibility in network architecture, with very little code.

Keras currently has two APIs for building models. In my examples, I'll be using the functional API. It's slightly more verbose but it allows additional flexibility. I'd recommend using the functional API whenever possible.

Our MLP will need an input layer, a hidden layer, and an output layer.

Input layer shape

Since we've already identified our inputs, we know that the input matrix will have a number of rows equal to the number of data elements/observations in our dataset and a number of columns equal to the number of variables/features. The shape of the input matrix then is (number of observations x 10 features). Rather than defining the exact number of records in our dataset or minibatch, TensorFlow and Keras allow us to use `None` as a placeholder when we define the number of elements in a dataset.

 If you see a None dimension used in a Keras or TensorFlow model layer shape, it really means any, the dimension could take on any positive integer value.

Hidden layer shape

Our hidden layer will start with 32 neurons. At this point, we can't know how many neurons are necessary. This is really a hyperparameter and can be explored and tuned later. Identifying an appropriate network architecture for a given problem is an open problem in the field of deep learning.

Since each of these 32 neurons in the hidden layer will output their activation to the output layer, the shape of the hidden layer will be (10, 32).

Output layer shape

Our final layer will consist of a single neuron that, using the 32 inputs from the hidden layer, will predict a single output value $\hat{y}$ for each observation.

Putting all the layers together, our MLP network structure will look like this:

| input: InputLayer | input: | (None, 10) |
| | output: | (None, 10) |

| hidden: Dense | input: | (None, 10) |
| | output: | (None, 32) |

| final: Dense | input: | (None, 32) |
| | output: | (None, 1) |

Neural network architecture

Now that we've defined the input and output, we can take a look at the code for the network.

```
from keras.layers import Input, Dense
from keras.models import Model
def build_network(input_features=None):
    inputs = Input(shape=(input_features,), name="input")
    x = Dense(32, activation='relu', name="hidden")(inputs)
    prediction = Dense(1, activation='linear', name="final")(x)
    model = Model(inputs=inputs, outputs=prediction)
    model.compile(optimizer='adam', loss='mean_absolute_error')
    return model
```

That's all there is to it! We can then use this code to build a neural network instance suitable for our problem simply by calling it, as follows:

```
model = build_network(input_features=10)
```

Before we get to that, however, let's review a few interesting parts of the preceding code:

- Every layer is *chained* to the layer above it. Every layer is callable and returns a tensor. For example, our hidden layer is *tied* to the input layer when the hidden layer calls it:

```
x = Dense(32, activation='relu', name="hidden")(inputs)
```

- Our final layer's activation function is linear. This is the same as not using any activation, which is what we want for regression.
- Keras models need to be compiled with `.compile()`.
- During the compile call, you need to define the cost function and optimizer you will use. I've used MAE for the cost function in this example, as we discussed. I used Adam with default parameters as my optimizer, which we covered a bit in chapter 1. It's likely that we will eventually want to tune Adam's learning rate. Doing so is quite simple: you just need to define a custom `adam` instance, and use that instead:

```
from keras.optimizers import Adam
adam_optimizer = Adam(lr=0.001, beta_1=0.9, beta_2=0.999, epsilon=1e-08,
decay=0.0)
model.compile(optimizer=adam_optimizer, loss='mean_absolute_error')
```

Training the Keras model

Now that our network has been built and compiled, all that's left is to train it. Much like in Python's scikit-learn, you can do that by calling `.fit()` on the model instance, as shown in the following code:

```
model.fit(x=data["train_X"], y=data["train_y"], batch_size=32, epochs=200,
verbose=1, validation_data=(data["val_X"], data["val_y"]))
```

Let us walk through a few of the important arguments the Keras fit method takes. I will assume that you're familiar with mini-batch gradient descent and training epochs but if you aren't, please check `Chapter 1`, *The Building Blocks of Deep Learning*, for an overview. The important arguments in the Keras fit model are as follows:

- `batch_size`: Keras defaults to a batch size of 32. The batch size is the size of the mini-batch Keras will use. Of course, this means that Keras assumes you want to use mini-batch gradient descent. If, for some reason, you don't want to use mini-batch gradient, you can set `batch_size=None`.
- `epochs`: An epoch is just a single pass over the entire training set. In practice, you'll need to monitor your network as it trains to learn when the network has converged, so `epochs` is a somewhat learnable hyperparameter. Later, we will see that it's possible to save the weights of our model every epoch, or even every epoch that's better than the last. Once we know how to do that, we can choose the epoch we think is best and implement a sort of human-based early stopping.

- `validation_data`: Here, we are specifying our validation set. At the end of every epoch, Keras will test the model on the validation set and output the results using the loss function and any other metrics you've specified. Alternatively, you can set `validation_split` to a float value specifying the percentage of the train set you'd like to use for validation. Both options work fine, but I prefer to be very explicit when it comes to dataset splits.
- `verbose`: This is somewhat self-explanatory; however, it merits a quick mention. `verbose=1` outputs a progress bar that shows the status of the current epoch and, at the end of the epoch, Keras will output training and validation loss. `verbose` can also be set to 2, which outputs loss information every mini-batch, and 0, which makes Keras silent.

Measuring the performance of our model

Now that our MLP has been trained, we can start to understand how good it is. I'll make a prediction on our `Train`, `Val`, and `Test` datasets to do so. The code for the same is as follows:

```
print("Model Train MAE: " + str(mean_absolute_error(data["train_y"],
model.predict(data["train_X"]))))
print("Model Val MAE: " + str(mean_absolute_error(data["val_y"],
model.predict(data["val_X"]))))
print("Model Test MAE: " + str(mean_absolute_error(data["test_y"],
model.predict(data["test_X"]))))
```

For our MLP, this is how well we did:

```
Model Train MAE: 0.190074701809
Model Val MAE: 0.213255747475
Model Test MAE: 0.199885450841
```

Keep in mind that our data has been scaled to 0 mean and unit variance. The `Train MAE` is `0.19`, and our `Val MAE` is `0.21`. These two errors are pretty close to each other, so over fitting isn't something I'd be too concerned about. Because I am expecting some amount of over fitting that I don't see (usually over fitting is the bigger problem), I hypothesize this model might have too much bias. Said another way, we might not be able to fit the data closely enough. When this occurs, we need to add more layers, more neurons, or both to our model. We need to go deeper. Let's do that next.

We can attempt to reduce network bias by adding parameters to the network, in the form of more neurons. While you might be tempted to start tuning your optimizer, it's usually better to find a network architecture you're comfortable with first.

Building a deep neural network in Keras

Changing our model is as easy as redefining our previous `build_network()` function. Our input layer will stay the same because our input hasn't changed. Likewise, the output layer should remain the same.

I'm going to add parameters to our network by adding additional hidden layers. I hope that by adding these hidden layers, our network can learn more complicated relationships between the input and output. I am going to start by adding four additional hidden layers; the first three will have 32 neurons and the fourth will have 16. Here's what it will look like:

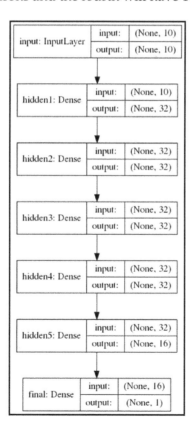

And here's the associated code for building the model in Keras:

```
def build_network(input_features=None):
    inputs = Input(shape=(input_features,), name="input")
    x = Dense(32, activation='relu', name="hidden1")(inputs)
    x = Dense(32, activation='relu', name="hidden2")(x)
    x = Dense(32, activation='relu', name="hidden3")(x)
    x = Dense(32, activation='relu', name="hidden4")(x)
    x = Dense(16, activation='relu', name="hidden5")(x)
    prediction = Dense(1, activation='linear', name="final")(x)
    model = Model(inputs=inputs, outputs=prediction)
    model.compile(optimizer='adam', loss='mean_absolute_error')
    return model
```

As promised, very little of our code has changed. I've bolded the additional lines. The rest of our code can stay the same; however, you often have to train longer (for more epochs) as network complexity increases.

Measuring the deep neural network performance

Is a deep network really better than an MLP on this problem? Let's find out! After training for 500 epochs, here's how the model performed:

```
Model Train MAE: 0.0753991873787
Model Val MAE: 0.189703853999
Model Test MAE: 0.190189985043
```

We can see that the `Train MAE` has now decreased from `0.19` to `0.075`. We've greatly reduced the bias of the network.

However, our variance has increased. The difference between the training error and validation error is much larger. Our `Val` set error did move down slightly, which is good; however, this large gap between training error and validation error suggests we are starting to over fit on the training set.

The most straightforward way to reduce variance in cases like this is to either add additional training data or apply a regularization technique such as L2 regularization or dropout, which we will cover in the next chapter.

More data is often the best fix for a high variance network. If it's possible to collect more data, that's probably the best place to spend your time.

Once a network has been built, I like to inspect the errors visually to get a feel for how well the network is modelling the validation set distribution. This often leads to insights that will help me improve the model. For a regression model, I like to plot a histogram of the predicted and actual values of the validation set. Let's see how well I did. The plot is as follows for your reference:

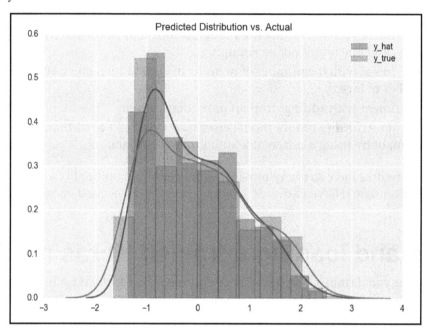

Overall, I think the model is predicting the actual distribution fairly closely. It appears that the actual validation dataset is shifted slightly more to the left (smaller values) than the predicted dataset, which may be an important insight. Said another way, the network may be predicting wines have more alcohol than they do on average, especially in the cases where alcohol is somewhat low. Examining the validation data more closely might suggest how we would go about collecting more training data.

Tuning the model hyperparameters

Now that we've trained an MLP and a six-layer deep neural network on the problem, we're ready to tune and optimize model hyperparameters.

We will discuss model tuning in depth in `Chapter 6`, *Hyperparameter Optimization*. There are a variety of strategies that you can use to choose the best parameters for your model. As you've probably noticed, there are many possible parameters and hyperparameters that we could still optimize.

If you wanted to fully tune this model you should do the following:

- Experiment with the number of hidden layers. It appears that five might be too many, and one might not be enough.
- Experiment with the number of neurons in each hidden layer, relative to the number of layers.
- Experiment with adding dropout or regularization.
- Attempt to further reduce model error by trying SGD or RMS prop instead of Adam, or by using a different learning rate for Adam.

Deep neural networks have so many moving parts, getting to optimal is sometimes an exhausting notion. You'll have to decide whether your model is good enough.

Saving and loading a trained Keras model

It's unlikely that you'll train a deep neural network and then apply it in the same script. Most likely, you will want to train your network and then save the structure and weights so that they can be used in a production-facing application designed to score new data. To do so, you'll need to be able to save and load your models.

Saving a model in Keras is very straightforward. You can use the model instance's `.save()` method to save the network structure and weights to an `hdf5` file, as shown in the following code:

```
model.save("regression_model.h5")
```

That's really all there is to it. Loading a model from disk is just as simple. The code for doing this is given here for your reference:

```
from keras.models import load_model
model = load_model("regression_model.h5")
```

Summary

When you think about deep learning, you probably think about impressively complex computer vision problems, but deep neural networks can prove useful even for simple regression problems like this one. Hopefully, I've demonstrated that, while also introducing the Keras syntax and showing you how to build a very simple network.

As we continue, we will encounter much more complexity. Bigger networks, more complicated cost functions, and highly dimensional input data. However, the process I used in this chapter will remain same for the most part. In each case, we will outline the problem, identify the inputs and outputs, choose a cost function, create a network architecture, and finally train and tune our model.

Bias and variance can often be manipulated and reduced independently in deep neural networks if the following factors are taken care of:

- **Bias**: This can be reduced by adding model complexity. Additional neurons or layers will help. Adding data won't really help reduce bias.
- **Variance**: This can be reduced by adding data or regularization.

In the next chapter, we will talk about how we can use TensorBoard to optimize and troubleshoot our deep neural networks faster.

3
Monitoring Network Training Using TensorBoard

In this chapter, I'm going to show you how to use TensorBoard to help make training your deep neural networks faster and easier. I think that TensorBoard is a great and often overlooked tool, which is far too often relegated to a footnote or the last chapter. Now, let's take a look at TensorBoard so we can start to take advantage of it right away.

We will be covering the following topics in this chapter:

- A brief overview of TensorBoard
- Setting up TensorBoard
- Connecting Keras to TensorBoard
- Using TensorBoard

A brief overview of TensorBoard

TensorBoard is a web-based application that can help you visualize the metrics, parameters, and structure of a deep neural network created in TensorFlow. It will help you debug and optimize your deep neural networks faster and easier.

As you've probably guessed by now, deep neural networks can get quite complex. That, unfortunately, means that there are quite a few things that can go wrong. I've been known to make a mistake every now and then, and when bugs happen inside a deep neural network, which is inside a framework, that runs on another framework, that runs on a GPU, it can be very hard to find these them. TensorBoard can be the flashlight you need to find the problem in an otherwise very dark room. TensorBoard will allow you to monitor the changes in metrics and parameters as your network is trained, which can greatly accelerate troubleshooting.

TensorBoard is also great for optimization. With TensorBoard, you can visually compare multiple model runs against each other. This allows you to experiment with changing architectures and hyperparameters and then evaluate those changes relative to the other runs of the network. All this can happen throughout each epoch, so you can kill model runs that aren't doing well early if you desire, which saves you time and money. You can read more about TensorBoard at `https://www.tensorflow.org/programmers_guide/summaries_and_tensorboard`.

Setting up TensorBoard

TensorBoard is a standalone web application. You'll use it through your web browser. The setup requires two steps. First, we will set up TensorBoard to visualize the networks that we build in TensorFlow and Keras, and then we will set up Keras to share information with TensorBoard.

This section covers the setup of TensorBoard. The next will cover modifying your Keras code to share information with TensorBoard.

Installing TensorBoard

If you've installed TensorFlow already, Tensorboard is probably already installed on your machine. Just in case you can install and update TensorBoard can be installed using `pip`, just like Keras and TensorFlow. To install it, just run the following:

```
pip install -U tensorboard
```

How TensorBoard talks to Keras/TensorFlow

TensorBoard and TensorFlow use a common log directory to share information. As Keras and TensorFlow train, Keras will write metrics and activation histograms (more on this soon) to the log directory you specify. For now, let's create a log directory for this example in our home directory, using the following code:

```
mkdir ~/ch3_tb_log
```

Running TensorBoard

All that's left is to start the TensorBoard process. We can start TensorBoard using the following code:

```
tensorboard --logdir ~/ch3_tb_log --port 6006
```

As you might have guessed, `--logdir` specifies the directory we just created and `--port` `6006` specifies the port that TensorBoard will run on. Port `6006` is the default; however, you can use whatever port you want.

You should now be able to navigate to the TensorBoard URL by pointing your browser at `http://<ip address>:6006`

If you're using a cloud service, you may also need to adjust a firewall or security rule to allow connects to your server on port `6006`. On Amazon Web Services (AWS), you can do this by editing the inbound rules in the security group associated with your EC2 instance:

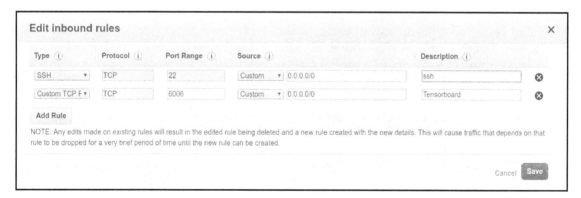

You may not want to allow the entire world open access, as I do above. This is just a test instance so I'm not too concerned with security and anyway I like to live dangerously.

If everything is working, you should see an empty TensorBoard as follows:

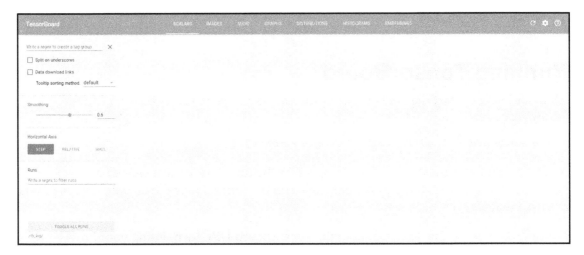

Don't worry, we will fill it up shortly.

Connecting Keras to TensorBoard

Now that TensorBoard is up and running, all that's left is to tell Keras to write TensorBoard logs to the directory we specified above. Luckily, this is really easy to do, and it gives us a great opportunity to learn about a special class of functions in Keras called **Keras callbacks**.

Introducing Keras callbacks

Callbacks in Keras are functions that can be run during the training process. They can do all kinds of great things, such as saving your model weights after an epoch, logging things, changing your hyperparameters, or conveniently writing TensorBoard log files. You can even create your own custom callbacks.

We will be using the TensorBoard callback in the next section; however, I'd encourage you to take a look at all the callbacks available in Keras at `https://keras.io/callbacks`.

TensorBoard callbacks are objects that can be configured and instantiated before model training. We will be creating a list of these callbacks. Once we have created a list of callbacks that we want to use with our deep neural network, we can simply pass that list as an argument to the model's `.fit()` method. These callbacks will then be used at each epoch, or as appropriate by Keras. This will make more sense as we walk through the next example.

Creating a TensorBoard callback

I've started us off in this chapter by copying our networks and data from Chapter 2, *Using Deep Learning to Solve Regression Problems*. We're going to make a few simple additions to add our TensorBoard callback. Let's start by modifying the `mlp` we built first.

First, we need to import the TensorBoard callback class, using the following code:

```
from keras.callbacks import TensorBoard
```

Then we will initiate the callback. I like to do this inside a function that creates all my callbacks, to keep things carefully crafted and tidy. The create_callbacks() function below will return a list of all the callbacks we will pass to `.fit()`. In this case, it returns a list with one element:

```
def create_callbacks():
    tensorboard_callback = TensorBoard(log_dir='~/ch3_tb_log/mlp',
        histogram_freq=1, batch_size=32, write_graph=True,
            write_grads=False)
    return [tensorboard_callback]
```

Before we move on, let's cover some of the arguments we're using here:

- `log_dir`: This is the path we will write the log files for TensorBoard.

You might have noticed that I'm writing logs for the MLP network's TensorBoard callback to `~/ch_3_tb_log/mlp`, which creates a new director `mlp` under the directory that we specified for TensorBoard. This is intentional. We will configure the deep neural network model we trained in `Chapter 2`, *Using Deep Learning to Solve Regression Problems*, to log to a separate directory, `~/ch_3_tb_log/dnn`. Doing so will allow us to compare both model runs against each other.

- `histogram_freq`: This specifies how often we will compute histograms for activations and weights (in epochs). It defaults to 0, which makes the log much smaller but doesn't generate histograms. We will cover why and when you'll be interested in histograms shortly.
- `batch_size`: This is the batch size used to calculate histograms. It defaults to 32.
- `write_graph`: This function is Boolean. This will tell TensorBoard to visualize the network graph. This can be quite handy, but it can also make the logs quite large.
- `write_grads`: This function is also Boolean. This will tell TensorBoard to calculate histograms of gradients as well.

Because TensorFlow automatically calculates gradients for you, this is rarely used. However, if you were to use custom activations or costs, it could be an excellent troubleshooting tool.

The TensorBoard callback can take additional arguments used for neural networks operating on images, or by using embedded layers. We will cover both later in the book. If you're interested in these features, please see the TensorBoard API doc at `https://keras.io/callbacks/#tensorboard`.

Now we just need to create our list of callbacks and fit our `mlp` with the `callbacks` argument. That will look like this:

```
callbacks = create_callbacks()
model.fit(x=data["train_X"], y=data["train_y"], batch_size=32,
  epochs=200, verbose=1, validation_data=(data["val_X"],
    data["val_y"]), callbacks=callbacks)
```

I've bolded the new argument for clarity.

Before we move on to using TensorBoard, I will instrument the deep neural network the same way I instrumented the `mlp`. The only change in code will be the directory we write TensorBoard logs to. The method for implementing the same is given below, for your reference:

```
def create_callbacks():
tensorboard_callback = TensorBoard(log_dir='./ch3_tb_log/dnn',
  histogram_freq=1, batch_size=32, write_graph=True, write_grads=False)
    return [tensorboard_callback]
```

The rest of the code will be the same. Now, let's train each network again and take a look at TensorBoard.

Using TensorBoard

Now that we've completely configured TensorBoard and told our networks how to send log data to it, we can start taking advantage of it. In the remainder of the chapter, I'm going to show you some of my favorite ways to use TensorBoard. There is more to TensorBoard than this, and we will revisit additional functionality throughout the remainder of the book.

Visualizing training

Since we've written log data from both the models in Chapter 2, *Using Deep Learning to Solve Regression Problems*, we can use TensorBoard to compare the two models graphically. Open up TensorBoard and head to the **SCALARS** tab. You should see something like this. You may need to click **loss** and **val_loss** to expand the graphs:

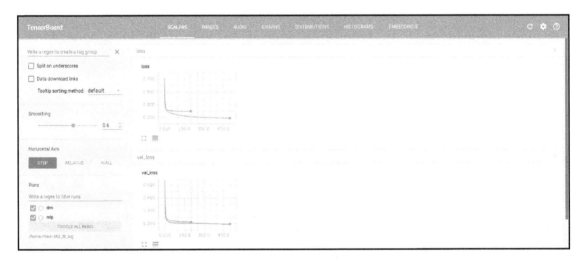

Tensorboard displaying the loss and val_loss plots for the model

If you look at the bottom-left corner of the screen, you should notice that each directory we created has a **run** associated with it. Both are currently selected. This means that on our graphs, we will see output for both models.

> TensorBoard can accommodate many, many runs, and you can filter them via a regular expression (for example ^dnn* would show all runs that start with dnn). This means that if you're searching for the *best* model through many experiments or runs (such as hyperparameter optimization), you can quickly navigate them if you explicitly and consistently name your runs and include meaningful hyperparameter and architecture information in the name, so do that!

The default **X** scale on these graphs is **epochs**. The **Y** value is the **loss function** we chose, which was **MAE**. You can click on the graphs to explore them and drag to zoom.

Seeing the graphs like this, we can really see the relative bias and variance of each network. While there is a good separation between the models in train loss, the deep neural network only gets marginally better on the validation set, suggesting that we've headed into overfitting territory.

Visualizing network graphs

While being able to see into our training process and comparing models is obviously pretty great, that's not all TensorBoard can do. We can also use it to visualize network structure. Here, I've navigated to **GRAPHS** and pulled up the structure of the deep neural network:

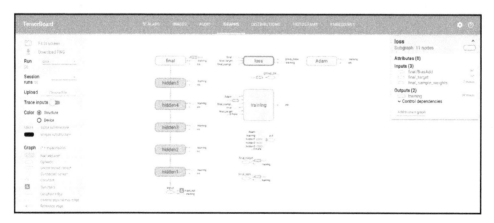

TensorBoard displaying the structure of the deep neural network

The **training** node represents the input tensor, and by default, it's this giant octopus that connects to the rest of the graph in a somewhat unhelpful way. To fix that, you can just click the node and click **Remove from the main graph**. It will then be moved off to the side.

Visualizing a broken network

TensorBoard is a great troubleshooting tool. To demonstrate this, I'm going to copy our deep neural network and break it! Luckily, breaking a neural network is really easy. Trust me, I've done it enough unintentionally that I'm basically an expert at this point.

Imagine that you have just trained a new neural network and seen that the loss looked like this:

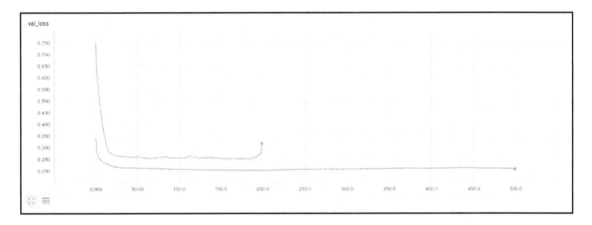

The loss function for this network is stuck, and it's way higher than our previous run. What went wrong?

Navigate to the **HISTOGRAMS** section of TensorBoard and visualize the first hidden layer. Let's compare the histogram of the weights for hidden layer 1 in both networks:

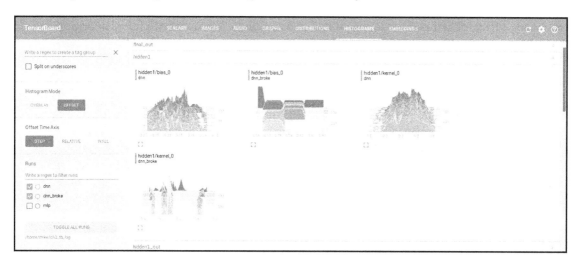

Sceenshot displaying the histogram of the weights for hidden layer 1 in both networks

For both the biases and weights of the network labelled **dnn**, you'll see that the weights are spread out across the graph. You might even say that the distribution of each could be normal(ish).

You can also compare the weights and biases in the distributions section. Both present mostly the same information in slightly different ways.

Now, look at the weight and biases of our broken network. Not *so spread out*, and in fact, the weights are all basically the same. The network isn't really learning. Every neuron in the layer appears to be more or less the same. If you look at the other hidden layers you'll see more of the same.

You might be wondering what I did to make this happen. You're in luck, I'll share my secret. After all, you never know when you might need to break your own network. To break things, I initialized every neuron in the network to the exact same value. When this happens, the error every neuron receives during backprop is exactly the same and changes exactly the same way. The network then fails to break symmetry. Initializing the weights to a deep neural network in a random way is really important, and this is what happens if you break that rule!

You can use TensorBoard exactly like this when you have a problem. Keep in mind our deep neural network has 4033, and that still qualifies as *tiny* in the world of deep learning. With TensorBoard, we were able to visually inspect 4033 parameters and identify a problem. TensorBoard is an amazing flashlight in the dark room that is deep learning.

Summary

In this chapter, we talked about how to install, configure, and use TensorBoard. We talked about how to use TensorBoard to compare models visually by inspecting their loss functions throughout each epoch in TensorBoard's **SCALARS** section. We then looked at visualizing the network structure using TensorsBoard's **GRAPHS** section. Finally, we showed you how to use TensorBoard for troubleshooting by looking at histograms.

In the next chapter, we will look how to use Keras and TensorFlow to solve binary classification problems, expanding our deep learning bag of tricks.

4
Using Deep Learning to Solve Binary Classification Problems

In this chapter, we will use Keras and TensorFlow to solve a tricky binary classification problem. We will start by talking about the benefits and drawbacks of deep learning for this type of problem, and then we will go right into developing a solution using the same framework we established in `Chapter 2`, *Using Deep Learning to Solve Regression Problems*. Finally, we will cover Keras callbacks in greater depth and even use a custom callback to implement a per epoch **receiver operating characteristic / area under the curve (ROC AUC)** metric.

We will cover the following topics in this chapter:

- Binary classification and deep neural networks
- Case study – epileptic seizure recognition
- Building a binary classifier in Keras
- Using the checkpoint callback in Keras
- Measuring ROC AUC in a custom callback
- Measuring precision, recall, and f1-score

Binary classification and deep neural networks

Binary classification problems, such as regression problems, are very common machine learning tasks. So much so that any book on deep learning wouldn't be complete without covering them. To be sure, we haven't really hit the sweet spot of deep neural networks quite yet, but we're well on our way. Before we get to the code, let's talk about the trade-offs you should consider when choosing a deep neural network to solve this kind of problem.

Benefits of deep neural networks

When compared to a more traditional classifier such as a logistic regression model, or even a tree-based model such as **random forest** or a **gradient boosting machine**, deep neural networks have a few nice advantages.

As with the regression we did in `Chapter 2`, *Using Deep Learning to Solve Regression Problems*, we don't need to select or screen features. In the problem that we have selected in this chapter, there are 178 input variables. Each input variable is a specific input from an **Electroencephalogram** (**EEG**) labelled **x1..x178**. Even if you were a medical doctor, it would be difficult to understand the relationship between that many features and the target variable. There is a good chance that some of those features are irrelevant, and a better chance that some higher-level interactions might exist between those variables and the target. If using a traditional model, we'd get the best model performance if we went through a feature selection step. That's not needed when using deep neural networks.

Drawbacks of deep neural networks

As we mentioned in `Chapter 2`, *Using Deep Learning to Solve Regression Problems*, deep neural networks aren't easily interpretable. While deep neural networks are wonderful predictors, it is not easy to understand why they arrived at the prediction they made. It bears repeating that when the task is to understand which features are most correlated with a change in the target, a deep neural network isn't the tool for the job. However, if the goal is raw predictive power, you should consider a deep neural network.

We should also give consideration to complexity. Deep neural networks are complex models with lots of parameters. Finding the best neural network can take time and experimentation. Not all problems warrant that level of complexity.

 In real life, I rarely use deep learning as my first solution to a structured data problem. I'll start with the simplest model that might possibly work, and then iterate to deep learning as the problem requires. When the problem domain contains images, audio, or text, I'm more likely to begin with deep learning.

Case study – epileptic seizure recognition

As you've probably guessed, we are going to be solving a binary classification problem. We will start by planning the problem using the same framework we established in Chapter 2, *Using Deep Learning to Solve Regression Problems*, and modify it as needed. You can find the complete code for this chapter in the book's GitHub repository, under Chapter 4, *Using Deep Learning to Solve Regression Problems*.

Defining our dataset

The dataset that we will be working on this chapter is called the **Epileptic Seizure Recognition** dataset. The data originally comes from a paper titled *Indications of nonlinear deterministic and finite dimensional structures in time series of brain electrical activity: Dependence on recording region and brain state* by Andrzejak RG and others, published in Phys. Rev. E, 64, 061907. You can find the data at the UCI machine learning repository at http://archive. ics.uci.edu/ml/datasets/Epileptic+Seizure+Recognition.

Our goal is to create a deep neural network that can predict whether the patient is having a seizure or not, given the input features.

Loading data

We can load the data used in this chapter with the following function. It's very similar to the function we used in chapter 2, however it's adapted for this dataset.

```
from sklearn.preprocessing import StandardScaler

def load_data():
  """Loads train, val, and test datasets from disk"""
```

```
train = pd.read_csv(TRAIN_DATA)
val = pd.read_csv(VAL_DATA)
test = pd.read_csv(TEST_DATA)

# we will use a dict to keep all this data tidy.
data = dict()
data["train_y"] = train.pop('y')
data["val_y"] = val.pop('y')
data["test_y"] = test.pop('y')

# we will use sklearn's StandardScaler to scale our data to 0 mean, unit
variance.
scaler = StandardScaler()
train = scaler.fit_transform(train)
val = scaler.transform(val)
test = scaler.transform(test)

data["train_X"] = train
data["val_X"] = val
data["test_X"] = test
# it's a good idea to keep the scaler (or at least the mean/variance) so
we can unscale predictions
data["scaler"] = scaler
return data
```

Model inputs and outputs

There are 11,500 rows in this dataset. Each row of the dataset contains 178 data points, each representing a 1-second sample of an EEG recording and a corresponding patient state, generated across 100 different patients.

There are five patient states in the dataset; however, patients in state 2 through state 5 were not experiencing a seizure. Patients in state 1 were experiencing a seizure.

I have modified the original dataset, reframing the problem into a binary classification problem by changing states 2-5 to class 0, which will mean no seizure and class 1, which will mean seizure.

As with the regression problem in Chapter 2, *Using Deep Learning to Solve Regression Problems*, we will be using an 80% train, 10% val, 10% test split.

The cost function

We need our classifier to predict the probability of seizure, which is class 1. This means that our output will be constrained to *[0,1]* as it would be in a traditional logistic regression model. Our cost function, in this case, will binary cross-entropy, which is also known as **log loss**. If you've worked with classifiers before, this math is likely familiar to you; however, as a refresher, I'll include it here.

The complete formula for log loss looks like this:

$$Cost = -\frac{1}{n} \sum_{i=1}^{n} [y_i \log \hat{y}_i + (1 - y_i) \log (1 - \hat{y}_i)]$$

This can probably be seen more simply as a set of two functions, one for case $y_i = 0$ and $y_i = 1$:

$$Cost = -\frac{1}{n} \sum_{i=1}^{n} \log (\hat{y}_i)$$

When $y_i = 1$ and

$$Cost = -\frac{1}{n} \sum_{i=1}^{n} \log (1 - \hat{y}_i)$$

When $y_i = 0$

The log function is used here to result in a monotonic function (one that is always increasing or decreasing) that we can easily differentiate. As with all cost functions, we will adjust our network parameters to minimize the cost of the network.

Using metrics to assess the performance

In addition to a `loss` function, Keras lets us also use metrics to help judge the performance of a model. While minimizing loss is good, it's not especially obvious how we expect the model to perform given some `loss` function. Metrics aren't used in training the model, they're just there to help us understand the current state.

While loss might not mean much to us, accuracy does. We humans understand accuracy fairly well.

Keras defines binary accuracy as follows:

```
def binary_accuracy(y_true, y_pred):
    return K.mean(K.equal(y_true, K.round(y_pred)), axis=-1)
```

This is really just a clever way to simply divide the number of correct answers by the total answers, as we've likely been doing since our very early days in school to figure out our grade on a test.

You might be wondering whether our dataset is balanced because accuracy works so poorly for unbalanced datasets. It's in fact not balanced. Only one-fifth of the dataset is class 1. We will calculate the ROC AUC score as a custom callback to address this. ROC isn't implemented in Keras as a metric because metrics are computed for every mini batch and the ROC AUC score isn't really defined by mini batch.

Building a binary classifier in Keras

Now that we've defined our problem, our inputs, our desired output, and our cost function, we can quickly code the rest in Keras. The only thing we're missing is a network architecture. We will talk more about that soon. One of my favorite things about Keras is how easy it is tune the network architecture. As you're about to see, it might take a lot of experimentation before you locate the best architecture. If that's true, a framework that easily changes makes your job easier!

The input layer

As before, our input layer needs to know the dimensions of our dataset. I like to build the entire Keras model inside a function, and allow that function to pass back the compiled model. Right now, this function only takes a single argument, the number of features. The following code is used to define the input layer:

```
def build_network(input_features=None):
    # first we specify an input layer, with a shape == features
    inputs = Input(shape=(input_features,), name="input")
```

The hidden layers

We've defined the input, that's the easy part. Now we need to decide on a network architecture. How can we know how many layers, and how many neurons we should include? I'd like to give you a formula. I really would. Unfortunately, it doesn't exist. In fact, some people are trying to build neural networks that can learn optimal architectures for other neural networks. For the rest of us, we will have to either experiment, search for ourselves, or borrow someone else's architecture.

What happens if we use too many neurons?

If we make our network architecture too complicated, two things will happen:

- We're likely to develop a high variance model
- The model will train slower than a less complicated model

If we add many layers, our gradients will get smaller and smaller until the first few layers barely train, which is called the **vanishing gradient problem**. We're nowhere near that yet, but we will talk about it later.

In (almost) the words of rap legend Christopher Wallace, aka Notorious B.I.G., the more neurons we come across, the more problems we see. With that said, the variance can be managed with dropout, regularization, and early stopping, and advances in GPU computing make deeper networks possible.

If I had to pick between a network with too many neurons or too few, and I only got to try one experiment, I'd prefer to err on the side of slightly too many.

What happens if we use too few neurons?

Imagine the case where we had no hidden layers and only an input and output. We talked about this architecture back in `Chapter 1`, *The Building Blocks of Deep Learning*, where we showed how it wouldn't be able to model the `XOR` function. Such a network architecture that wouldn't be able to model any nonlinearities in the data couldn't be modeled by the network. Each hidden layer presents an opportunity for feature engineering more and more complex interactions.

If you choose too few neurons, the outcome will likely be as follows:

- A really fast neural network
- That has high bias and doesn't predict very well

Choosing a hidden layer architecture

So now that we understand the price and behavior of choosing too many parameters and conversely not enough parameters, where do we start? To the best of my knowledge, all that's left is experimentation.

Measuring those experiments can be tricky. If your network trains quickly, like our early networks, then something like cross-validation can be implemented across a variety of architectures to evaluate multiple runs of each. If your network takes a long time to train, you might be left with something less statistically sophisticated. We will cover network optimization in `Chapter 6`, *Hyperparameter Optimization*.

> Some books have offered a rule of thumb for choosing a neural network architecture. I remain skeptical and unconvinced of such claims and you certainly won't find one here.

Coding the hidden layers for our example

For our example problem, I'll use five hidden layers because I think there are lots of interactions between features. My hunch is primarily based on domain knowledge. Having read the data description, I know this is a cross-sectional slice of a time series and maybe auto correlated.

I'll start with 128 neurons on the first layer (slightly fewer than my input size) and then collapse down to 16 by halves as we get toward the output. This isn't at all a rule of thumb, it's based on my own experience alone. We will use the following code to define our hidden layers:

```
x = Dense(128, activation='relu', name="hidden1")(inputs)
x = Dense(64, activation='relu', name="hidden2")(x)
x = Dense(64, activation='relu', name="hidden3")(x)
x = Dense(32, activation='relu', name="hidden4")(x)
x = Dense(16, activation='relu', name="hidden5")(x)
```

In each layer, I used `relu` activation, as it's usually the best and safest choice, but to be sure this is also a hyperparameter that can be experimented with.

The output layer

And finally, we need an output layer for our network. We will use the following code to define our output layer:

```
prediction = Dense(1, activation='sigmoid', name="final")(x)
```

We're building a binary classifier in this example, so we want our network to output the probability the observation belongs to class 1. Luckily, the `sigmoid` activation will do exactly that, constraining the network output to be between 0 and 1.

Putting it all together

Putting all that code together, all that's left is to compile our Keras model, specifying `binary_crossentrophy` as our `loss` function and `accuracy` as a metric we'd like to monitor through the training process. We will use the following code to compile our Keras model:

```
def build_network(input_features=None):
    inputs = Input(shape=(input_features,), name="input")
    x = Dense(128, activation='relu', name="hidden1")(inputs)
    x = Dense(64, activation='relu', name="hidden2")(x)
    x = Dense(64, activation='relu', name="hidden3")(x)
    x = Dense(32, activation='relu', name="hidden4")(x)
    x = Dense(16, activation='relu', name="hidden5")(x)
    prediction = Dense(1, activation='sigmoid', name="final")(x)
    model = Model(inputs=inputs, outputs=prediction)
    model.compile(optimizer='adam', loss='binary_crossentropy',
    metrics=["accuracy"])
```

```
return model
```

Training our model

Now that we've defined our model, we're all set to train it. Here's how we do that:

```
input_features = data["train_X"].shape[1]
model = build_network(input_features=input_features)
model.fit(x=data["train_X"], y=data["train_y"], batch_size=32, epochs=20,
verbose=1, validation_data=(data["val_X"], data["val_y"]),
callbacks=callbacks)
```

This should look pretty familiar if you've already read Chapter 2, *Using Deep Learning to Solve Regression Problems*. It's really, for the most part, the same. The callback list contains the TensorBoard callback, so let's watch our network train for 20 epochs and see what happens:

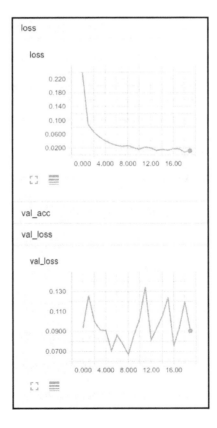

While our train loss continues to go mostly down, we can see that our **val_loss** is jumping all over the place. We're overfitting after about the eighth epoch.

There are several ways that we can reduce the variance in our network and manage this overfitting, and we will cover most of those methods in the next chapter. Before we do, however, I want to show you something useful called the **checkpoint callback**.

Using the checkpoint callback in Keras

In Chapter 2, *Using Deep Learning to Solve Regression Problems*, we saw the .save() method, that allowed us to save our Keras model after we were done training. Wouldn't it be nice, though, if we could write our weights to disk every now and then so that we could *go* back in time in the preceding example and save a version of the model before it started to overfit? We could then stop right there and use the lowest variance version of the network.

That's exactly what the ModelCheckpoint callback does for us. Let's take a look:

```
checkpoint_callback = ModelCheckpoint(filepath="./model-
weights.{epoch:02d}-{val_acc:.6f}.hdf5", monitor='val_acc', verbose=1,
save_best_only=True)
```

What ModelCheckpoint will do for us is save our model at scheduled intervals. Here, we are telling ModelCheckpoint to save a copy of the model every time we hit a new best validation accuracy (val_acc). We could have also monitored validation loss or any other metric we had specified.

The filename string will include the epoch number and the validation accuracy of the run.

When we train our model again, we can see these files being created:

```
model-weights.00-0.971304.hdf5
model-weights.02-0.977391.hdf5
model-weights.05-0.985217.hdf5
```

So, we can see that after epoch 5, we weren't able to best our val_acc, and no checkpoints were written. We could then go back and load the weights from checkpoint 5 and use our best model.

There are some big assumptions here in calling epoch 5 the best. You may want to run the network several times, especially if your dataset is relatively small, as it is with our early examples in this book. We can be fairly certain that this result won't be stable.

This is, by the way, a really simple way to prevent over fitting. We can just choose to use a checkpoint of the model that occurred before variance got too big. It's one way to do something like early stopping which means we stop training before the specified number of epochs when we see the model isn't improving.

Measuring ROC AUC in a custom callback

Let's use one more callback. This time, we will build a custom callback that computes Receiver Operating Characteristic Area Under the Curve (ROC AUC) at the end of every epoch, on both training and testing sets.

Creating a custom callback in Keras is actually really simple. All we need to do is create a class, inherent `Callback`, and override the method we need. Since we want to calculate the ROC AUC score at the end of each epoch, we will override on _epoch_end:

```
from keras.callbacks import Callback

class RocAUCScore(Callback):
    def __init__(self, training_data, validation_data):
        self.x = training_data[0]
        self.y = training_data[1]
        self.x_val = validation_data[0]
        self.y_val = validation_data[1]
        super(RocAUCScore, self).__init__()

    def on_epoch_end(self, epoch, logs={}):
        y_pred = self.model.predict(self.x)
        roc = roc_auc_score(self.y, y_pred)
        y_pred_val = self.model.predict(self.x_val)
        roc_val = roc_auc_score(self.y_val, y_pred_val)
        print('\n  *** ROC AUC Score: %s - roc-auc_val: %s ***' %
          (str(roc), str(roc_val)))
        return
```

Now that we've created our new custom callback, we can just add it to our callback creator function, as shown in the following code:

```
def create_callbacks(data):
    tensorboard_callback = TensorBoard(log_dir=os.path.join(os.getcwd(),
      "tb_log", "5h_adam_20epochs"), histogram_freq=1, batch_size=32,
        write_graph=True, write_grads=False)
    roc_auc_callback = RocAUCScore(training_data=(data["train_X"],
      data["train_y"]), validation_data=(data["val_X"], data["val_y"]))
```

```
checkpoint_callback = ModelCheckpoint(filepath="./model-weights.
    {epoch:02d}-{val_acc:.6f}.hdf5", monitor='val_acc',verbose=1,
save_best_only=True)
    return [tensorboard_callback, roc_auc_callback, checkpoint_callback]
```

That's all there is to it! You can implement any other metric you'd like in the same way.

Measuring precision, recall, and f1-score

As you're likely experienced with other binary classifiers, I thought it was wise to take a few sentences to talk about how to create some of the normal metrics used with more traditional binary classifiers.

One difference between the Keras functional API and what you might be used to in scikit-learn is the behavior of the `.predict()` method. When using Keras, `.predict()` will return an $n\times k$ matrix of k class probabilities for each of the n classes. For a binary classifier, there will be only one column, the class probability for class 1. This makes the Keras `.predict()` more like the `.predict_proba()` in scikit-learn.

When calculating precision, recall, or other class-based metrics, you'll need to transform the `.predict()` output by choosing some operating point, as shown in the following code:

```
def class_from_prob(x, operating_point=0.5):
    x[x >= operating_point] = 1
    x[x < operating_point] = 0
    return x
```

After you've done that, you are free to reuse the typical metrics found in `sklearn.metric`, as given in the following code:

```
y_prob_val = model.predict(data["val_X"])
y_hat_val = class_from_prob(y_prob_val)
print(classification_report(data["val_y"], y_hat_val))
```

Summary

In this chapter, we talked about using deep neural networks as binary classifiers. We spent quite a bit of time talking about network architecture design choices and touched on the idea that searching and experimentation is the best current way to choose an architecture.

We learned how to use the checkpoint callback in Keras to give us the power to go back in time and find a version of the model that has performance characteristics we like. Then we created and used a custom callback to measure ROC AUC score as the model trained. We wrapped up by looking at how to use the Keras `.predict()` method with traditional metrics from `sklearn.metrics`.

In the next chapter, we'll take a look at multiclass classification, and we will talk more about how to prevent over fitting in the process.

5
Using Keras to Solve Multiclass Classification Problems

In this chapter, we will use Keras and TensorFlow to take on a 10-class multiclass classification problem with lots of independent variables. As before, we will talk about the pros and cons of using deep learning for this problem; however, you won't find many cons. Lastly, we will spend a good amount of time talking about methods to control overfitting.

We will cover the following topics in this chapter:

- Multiclass classification and deep neural networks
- Case study – handwritten digit classification
- Building a multiclass classifier in Keras
- Controlling variance with dropout
- Controlling variance with regularization

Multiclass classification and deep neural networks

Here it is! We've finally gotten to the fun stuff! In this chapter, we will be creating a deep neural network that can classify an observation into multiple classes, and this is one of those places where neural networks really do well. Let's talk just a bit more about the benefit of deep neural networks for this class of problems.

Just so we're all talking about the same thing, let's define multiclass classification before we begin. Imagine we had a classifier that had, as inputs, the weights of various fruits and would predict the fruit given the weight. The output might be exactly one class in a set of classes (apple, banana, mango, and so on). That's multiclass classification, not to be confused with multilabel, which is the situation where a model might predict whether or not a set of labels will apply to the observations that aren't mutually exclusive.

Benefits

When there are a large number of classes we need to predict, deep neural networks are really great performers relative to other models. When the number of features in the input vector grows large, neural networks are a natural fit. When both of those situations converge on the same problem, a neural network might be where I started. That's exactly the type of problem we will see in the case study we will be working on this chapter.

Drawbacks

As before, a simpler model might do the job as well or better than a deep learning model. All else being equal, you should probably favor the simpler model. However, the cons of deep neural network complexity will often diminish as the number of classes increases. In order to accommodate many classes, many other models have to become significantly more complex in their implementation and some may even require you optimizing the multiclass strategy used for the model as a hyperparameter.

Case study - handwritten digit classification

We will be using a multiclass classification network to recognize the corresponding class of a handwritten digit. As before, you can find the complete code for this chapter in the book's Git repository, under Chapter05, if you'd like to follow along.

Problem definition

The `MNIST` dataset has become an almost canonical neural network dataset. This dataset consists of images of 60,000 handwritten digits, belonging to 10 classes representing their respective digit (0,1,2...9). Because this dataset has become so common, many deep learning frameworks come with an MNIST loading method built into the API. Both TensorFlow and Keras have one, and we will be using the Keras MNIST loader to make our lives a little easier. However, should you want to obtain the data from its original source, or perhaps learn more about MNIST's history, you can find more at `http://yann.lecun.com/exdb/mnist/`.

Model inputs and outputs

Our dataset has already been divided into a training set that is 50,000 observations large and a test set that is 10,000 observations large. I'll take the last 5,000 observations from the training set and use that as my validation set.

Flattening inputs

Each input observation is a 28 pixel by 28 pixel black and white image. An image like this one is represented on disk as a 28x28 matrix of values between 0 and 255, where each value is the intensity of black in that pixel. At this point, we only know how to train networks on two-dimensional vectors (we will learn a better way to do this later); so we will flatten this 28x28 matrix into a 1 x 784 input vector.

Once we stack all those 1x784 vectors, we are left with a 50,000 x 784 training set.

If you are experienced with convolutional neural networks, you're probably rolling your eyes right now, and if you aren't, you'll see a way better way to do this soon, but don't skip this chapter too fast. I think that a flattened `MNIST` is a really great dataset because it looks and behaves a lot like many of the complex real-life problems we encounter in domains with many inputs (for example, IoT, manufacturing, biological, pharma, and medical use cases).

Categorical outputs

Our output layer will contain a neuron for each class. Each class's associated neuron will be trained to predict the probability of that class as a value between 0 and 1. We will use a special activation called **softmax** to make sure all these outputs sum to one, and we will cover the details of softmax shortly.

This means that we will need to create a binary/categorical encoding of our classes. For example, if we had y = [0, 3, 2,1] and we encoded it categorically, we would have a matrix y like this:

$$y = \begin{bmatrix} 1 & 0 & 0 & 0 \\ 0 & 0 & 0 & 1 \\ 0 & 0 & 1 & 0 \\ 0 & 1 & 0 & 0 \end{bmatrix}$$

Luckily, Keras provides a convenient function to make this conversion for us.

Cost function

The cost function we will be using is called **multinomial cross-entropy**. Multinomial cross-entropy is really just a generalization of the binary cross-entropy function that we saw in `Chapter 4`, *Using Keras for Binary Classification*.

Instead of just showing you categorical cross-entropy, let's look at them both together. I'm going to assert they are equal, and then explain why:

$$Cost = -\frac{1}{n}\sum_{i=1}^{n}[y_i log(p_i) + (1 - y_i)]log(1 - p_i)] = -\frac{1}{n}\sum_{i=1}^{n}\sum_{j=1}^{m}[y_{ij}log(p_{ij})]$$

The preceding equation is true (when *m*=2)

OK, don't freak out. I know, that's a whole bunch of math. The categorical cross-entropy equation is the one that exists all the way on the right. Binary cross-entropy is next to it. Now, imagine a situation where *m*=2. In this case you can probably see that summing $y_{ij}log(p_{ij})$ for both *j* = 0 and *j* = 1, for each value in *i* would be equal to the result you'd get from binary cross-entropy. Hopefully that reduction is enough to make sense of categorical cross-entropy. If not, I'd suggest picking a few values and coding it up. It will only take a second and you'll thank me later!

Metrics

Categorical cross-entropy is a great cost function, but it doesn't actually tell us much about the quality of predictions we can expect from our network. Unfortunately, binary classifications metrics like ROC AUC don't help us much either, as we move beyond binary classification AUC isn't really defined.

Given the lack of a better metric, I'll be using accuracy as a human understandable training metric. Luckily, in this case, my dataset is balanced. Accuracy is defined, as you'd expect, at the number of times the true value matches the predicted value, divided by the total dataset size.

After training is complete, I'll be using scikit-learn's classification report to show us the precision and recall for each class individually. If you like, you could also use a confusion matrix for this.

Building a multiclass classifier in Keras

Since we now have a well-defined problem, we can start to code it. As we mentioned earlier, we have to make a few transformations to our inputs and outputs this time. I'll show you those here as we're building the network.

Loading MNIST

Luckily for us, an MNIST loading function that retrieves the MNIST data and loads it for us is built right into Keras. All we need to do is import `keras.datasets.mnist` and use the `load_data()` method, as shown in the following code:

```
(train_X, train_y), (test_X, test_y) = mnist.load_data()
```

The shape of `train_X` is 50,000 x 28 x 28. As we explained in the *Model inputs and outputs* section, we will need to flatten the 28x28 matrix into a 784 element vector. NumPy makes that pretty easy. The following code illustrates this technique:

```
train_X = train_X.reshape(-1, 784)
```

With that out of the way, we should think about scaling the input. Previously, we used scikit-learn's `StandardScaler`. There's no need to do so with MNIST. Since we know every pixel is in the same range, from 0 to 255, we can easily convert the value to between 0 and 1 by dividing by 255, explicitly casting the data type to `float32` before we do it, as shown in the following code:

```
train_X = train_X.astype('float32')
train_X /= 255
```

While we're loading data, we should probably convert our dependent variable vectors to categorical ones, as we talked about in the *Model inputs and outputs* section. To do so, we will use `keras.utils.to_categorical()`, with the help of the following code:

```
train_y = to_categorical(train_y)
```

With that, our data is now ready for training!

Input layer

Our input layer is actually unchanged from previous examples, but I'll include it here to make this a proper quick reference:

```
def build_network(input_features=None):
    inputs = Input(shape=(input_features,), name="input")
```

Hidden layers

I'm going to use a first hidden layer with 512 neurons. That's slightly smaller than the input vector's 784 elements, but that's not at all a rule. Again, this architecture is just a start and isn't necessarily best. I'll then walk down the size through the second and third hidden layers, as shown in the following code:

```
x = Dense(512, activation='relu', name="hidden1")(inputs)
x = Dense(256, activation='relu', name="hidden2")(x)
x = Dense(128, activation='relu', name="hidden3")(x)
```

Output layer

Our output layer will contain 10 neurons, one for each of the possible classes that an observation might be a member of. This corresponds to the encoding we imposed when we used `to_categorical()` on the y vectors:

```
prediction = Dense(10, activation='softmax', name="output")(x)
```

As you can see, the activation we're using is called **softmax**. Let's talk about what `softmax` is, and why it's useful.

Softmax activation

Imagine if, instead of a deep neural network, we were using k logistic regressions, where each regression is predicting membership in a single class. That collection of logistic regressions, one for each class would look like this:

$$f(x) = \begin{cases} P(Y=0) = sigmoid(\theta_0 * X) \\ P(Y=1) = sigmoid(\theta_1 * X) \\ P(Y=2) = sigmoid(\theta_2 * X) \\ P(Y=k) = sigmoid(\theta_k * X) \end{cases}$$

The problem with using this group of logistic regressions is that the output of each individual logistic regression is independent. Imagine a case where several of these logistic regressions in our set were uncertain of membership in their particular class, resulting in multiple answers that were around $P(Y=k) = 0.5$. This keeps us from using these outputs as an overall probability of class membership across the k classes because they won't necessarily sum to 1.

Softmax helps us by squeezing the outputs of all these logistic regressions such that they sum to 1 and the outputs can be used as an overall class membership probability.

The `softmax` function looks like this:

$$\sigma(z)_j = \frac{e^{z_j}}{\sum_{k=1}^{K} e^{z_k}}$$

(for j = classes 1 to k, and where zj/zk is the logistic regression belonging to that k)

So then, if we place the `softmax` function in front of our previous set of regressions, we get a set of class probabilities that conveniently sum to 1 and can be used as probability of class membership across the k classes. That changes our overall function to look like this:

$$P(Y = k) = softmax \begin{cases} P(Y = 0) = sigmoid(\theta_0 * X) \\ P(Y = 1) = sigmoid(\theta_1 * X) \\ P(Y = 2) = sigmoid(\theta_2 * X) \\ P(Y = k) = sigmoid(\theta_k * X) \end{cases}$$

The preceding function is often called multinomial logistic regression. It's sort of like a one layer, output only, and neural network. We don't use multinomial logistic regression frequently anymore; however, we most certainly use the `softmax` function all the time. For most multiclass classification problems in the book, we will be using `softmax`, so it's worth understanding.

If you're like me, and you find all that math hard to read, it might be easier to look at `softmax` in code. So, let's do that before we move on, with the following code snippet:

```
def softmax(z):
  z_exp = [math.exp(x) for x in z]
  sum_z_exp = sum(z_exp)
  softmax = [round(i / sum_z_exp, 3) for i in z_exp]
  return softmax
```

Let's quickly try an example. Imagine we had a set of logistic outputs that looked like this:

```
z = np.array([0.9, 0.8, 0.2, 0.1, 0.5])
```

If we apply `softmax`, we can easily convert these outputs to relative class probabilities, like this:

```
print(softmax(z))
[0.284, 0.257, 0.141, 0.128, 0.19]
```

Putting it all together

Now that we've covered the individual pieces, let's take a look at our overall network. This looks similar to the models we've previously covered in the book. However, we're using the loss function `categorical_crossentropy`, which we covered in the *Cost function* section of this chapter.

We will define our network using the following code:

```
def build_network(input_features=None):
    # first we specify an input layer, with a shape == features
    inputs = Input(shape=(input_features,), name="input")
    x = Dense(512, activation='relu', name="hidden1")(inputs)
    x = Dense(256, activation='relu', name="hidden2")(x)
    x = Dense(128, activation='relu', name="hidden3")(x)
    prediction = Dense(10, activation='softmax', name="output")(x)
    model = Model(inputs=inputs, outputs=prediction)
    model.compile(optimizer='adam', loss='categorical_crossentropy',
metrics=["accuracy"])
    return model
```

Training

Now that we've defined our neural network and loaded our data, all that's left is to train it.

In this, and several other examples throughout the book I'm using a dictionary called data to pass around the various datasets such as train_X, val_X, and test_X. I use this notation to keep the code readable, and because passing the entire dictionary is necessary more often than not.

Here's how I will train the model we've just built.

```
model = build_network(data["train_X"].shape[1])
model.fit(x=data["train_X"], y=data["train_y"],
          batch_size=30,
          epochs=50,
          validation_data=(data["val_X"], data["val_y"]),
          verbose=1,
          callbacks=callbacks)
```

I'm using the same callbacks that we've previously used. I'm not using the ROC AUC callback we built in Chapter 4, *Using Keras for Binary Classification*, as ROC AUC isn't clearly defined for multiclass classifiers.

Some creative solutions to this problem exist; for example, **Approximating the multiclass ROC by pairwise analysis** (http://citeseerx.ist.psu.edu/viewdoc/download?doi=10.1.1.108.3250rep=rep1type=pdf) and **Volume under the ROC surface** (http://citeseerx.ist.psu.edu/viewdoc/download?doi=10.1.1.14.2427rep=rep1type=pdf) are great papers that both address the problem. However, in practice, these methods and their metrics are rarely used and most commonly implemented in R. So, for now, let's stick with multiclass accuracy and stay far away from R.

Let's watch TensorBoard as our model trains:

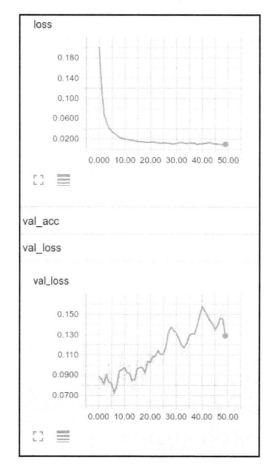

Before you read the next paragraph, take a second and think about what these graphs are telling us. Got it? OK, let's move on.

So, this is a familiar situation. Our training loss is continuing to creep down, while our validation loss is going up. We're overfitting. While early stopping is certainly an option, let me show you a few new tricks to handle overfitting. Let's look at dropout and l2 regularization in the next section. Before we do, however, we should look at how to measure accuracy and make predictions using a multiclass network.

Using scikit-learn metrics with multiclass models

As before, we can borrow metrics from scikit-learn to measure our model. To do so, however, we will need to make some easy conversions from the model's categorical output of y, as scikit-learn expects class labels, not binary class indicators.

To make the leap, we will start by making our prediction, using the following code:

```
y_softmax = model.predict(data["test_X"])
```

Then, we will choose the index of the class with the largest probability, which will conveniently be the class using the following code:

```
y_hat = y_softmax.argmax(axis=-1)
```

Then, we can use scikit-learn's classification report, as before. The code for the same is as follows:

```
from sklearn.metrics import classification_report
print(classification_report(test_y, y_hat))
```

We can actually look at the precision, recall, and f1-score for all 10 classes now. The following figure illustrates the output from `sklearn.metrics.classification_report()`:

```
model test loss is 0.096906474605 accuracy is 0.9806
             precision    recall  f1-score   support

          0       0.99      0.99      0.99       980
          1       0.99      0.99      0.99      1135
          2       0.99      0.97      0.98      1032
          3       0.99      0.98      0.99      1010
          4       0.98      0.98      0.98       982
          5       0.99      0.97      0.98       892
          6       0.98      0.99      0.98       958
          7       0.98      0.98      0.98      1028
          8       0.95      0.97      0.96       974
          9       0.97      0.97      0.97      1009

avg / total       0.98      0.98      0.98     10000
```

Controlling variance with dropout

One really great way to reduce overfitting in deep neural networks is to employ a technique called **dropout**. Dropout does exactly what it says, it drop neurons out of a hidden layer. Here's how it works.

Through every minibatch, we will randomly choose to turn off nodes in each hidden layer. Imagine we had some hidden layer where we had implemented dropout, and we chose the drop probability to be 0.5. That means, for every mini batch, for every neuron, we flip a coin to see whether we use that neuron. In doing so, you'd probably randomly turn off about half of the neurons in that hidden layer:

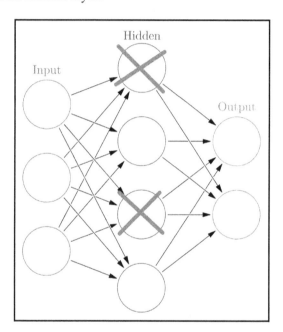

If we do this over and over again, it's like we're training many smaller networks. The model weights remain relatively smaller, and each smaller network is less likely to overfit the data. It also forces each neuron to be less dependent on the other neurons doing their jobs.

Dropout works amazingly well to combat overfitting on many, if not most, of the deep learning problems that you are likely to encounter. If you have a high variance model, dropout is a good first choice to reduce overfitting.

Keras contains a built in Dropout layer that we can easily use to implement Dropout in the network. A Dropout layer will simply turn off the outputs to neurons in the previous layer, randomly, to let us easily retrofit our network to use Dropout. To use it, we will need to first import the new layer in addition to the other layer types we're using, as shown in the following code:

```
from keras.layers import Input, Dense, Dropout
```

Then, we just insert Dropout layers into our model, as shown in the following code:

```
def build_network(input_features=None):
    # first we specify an input layer, with a shape == features
    inputs = Input(shape=(input_features,), name="input")
    x = Dense(512, activation='relu', name="hidden1")(inputs)
    x = Dropout(0.5)(x)
    x = Dense(256, activation='relu', name="hidden2")(x)
    x = Dropout(0.5)(x)
    x = Dense(128, activation='relu', name="hidden3")(x)
    x = Dropout(0.5)(x)
    prediction = Dense(10, activation='softmax', name="output")(x)
    model = Model(inputs=inputs, outputs=prediction)
    model.compile(optimizer='adam', loss='categorical_crossentropy',
                  metrics=["accuracy"])
    return model
```

This is the exact model we've previously used; however, we've inserted a Dropout layer after each Dense layer, which is how I normally start when I implement dropout. Like other model architecture decisions, you could choose to implement dropout in only some layers, all layers, or no layers. You can also choose to vary the dropout/keep probability; however, I do recommend starting at 0.5 as it tends to work pretty well.

A safe choice is dropout at every layer with keep probability 0.5. A good second try would be only using dropout at the first layer.

Let's train our new model with dropout, and see how it compares to our first try:

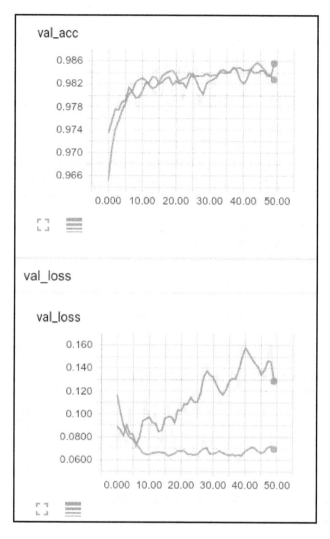

Let's take a look at validation accuracy first. The model using dropout struggles to train as fast as the unregularized model, but in this case, it does seem to get up to speed pretty quickly. Look at the validation accuracy at around epoch 44. It's marginally better than the unregularized model.

Now, let's look at validation loss. You can see the impact dropout had on the model overfitting and it's really quite pronounced. While it only translates to a marginal improvement in the final product, dropout is doing a pretty good job of keeping our validation loss from climbing.

Controlling variance with regularization

Regularization is another way to control overfitting, that penalizes individual weights in the model as they grow larger. If you're familiar with linear models such as linear and logistic regression, it's exactly the same technique applied at the neuron level. Two flavors of regularization, called L1 and L2, can be used to regularize neural networks. However, because it is more computationally efficient L2 regularization is almost always used in neural networks.

Quickly, we need to first regularize our cost function. If we imagine C_0, categorical cross-entropy, as the original cost function, then the regularized `cost` function would be as follows:

$$C = C_0 + \frac{\lambda}{2n} \sum_w w^2$$

Here, $;\lambda$ is a regularization parameter that can be increased or decreased to change the amount of regularization applied. This regularization parameter penalizes big values for weights, resulting in a network that hopefully has smaller weights overall.

For a more in-depth coverage of regularization in neural networks, check out Chapter 3 of Michael Nielsen's *Neural Networks and Deep Learning* at `http://neuralnetworksanddeeplearning.com/chap3.html`.

Regularization can be applied to the weights, biases, and activations in a Keras layer. I'll demonstrate this technique using L2, with the default parameters. In the following example I've applied regularization to each hidden layer:

```
def build_network(input_features=None):
    # first we specify an input layer, with a shape == features
    inputs = Input(shape=(input_features,), name="input")
    x = Dense(512, activation='relu', name="hidden1",
kernel_regularizer='l2') \
        (inputs)
    x = Dense(256, activation='relu', name="hidden2",
kernel_regularizer='l2')(x)
    x = Dense(128, activation='relu', name="hidden3",
```

```
kernel_regularizer='12')(x)
    prediction = Dense(10, activation='softmax', name="output")(x)
    model = Model(inputs=inputs, outputs=prediction)
    model.compile(optimizer='adam', loss='categorical_crossentropy',
                metrics=["accuracy"])
    return model
```

So, let's compare default L2 regularization to our other two models. The following figure shows the comparison:

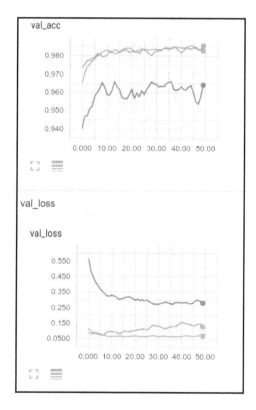

Our new L2 regularized network is unfortunately easy to spot. In this case, it seems that L2 regularization works a little too well. Our network is now high bias and hasn't learned as much as the other two.

If I were really determined to use regularization for this problem, I would start by changing the regularization rate and attempting to find a more suitable value, but we're so far off I'm skeptical that we will be successful in doing better than our dropout model.

Summary

In this chapter, we've really started to see just how powerful a deep neural network can be when doing multiclass classification. We covered the `softmax` function in detail and then we built and trained a network to classify handwritten digits into their 10 respective classes.

Finally, when we noticed that our model was overfitting, we attempted to use both dropout and L2 regularization to reduce the variance of the model.

By now, you've seen that deep neural networks require lots of choices, choices about architecture, learning rate, and even regularization rates. We will spend the next chapter learning how to optimize these choices.

6
Hyperparameter Optimization

One of the biggest drawbacks to using deep neural networks is that they have many hyperparameters that should be optimized so that the network performs optimally. In each of the earlier chapters, we've encountered, but not covered, the challenge of hyperparameter estimation. Hyperparameter optimization is a really big topic; it's, for the most part, an unsolved problem and, while we can't cover the entire topic in this book, I think it still deserves its own chapter.

In this chapter, I'm going to offer you what I believe is some practical advice for choosing hyperparameters. To be sure, this chapter may be somewhat opinionated and biased because it comes from my own experience. I hope that experience might be useful while also leading you to greater investigation on the topic.

We will cover the following topics in this chapter:

- Should network architecture be considered a hyperparameter?
- Which hyperparameters should we optimize?
- Hyperparameter optimization strategies

Should network architecture be considered a hyperparameter?

In building even the simplest network, we have to make all sorts of choices about network architecture. Should we use 1 hidden layer or 1,000? How many neurons should each layer contain? Should they all use the `relu` activation function or `tanh`? Should we use dropout on every hidden layer, or just the first? There are many choices we have to make in designing a network architecture.

In the most typical case, we search exhaustively for optimal values for each hyperparameter. It's not so easy to exhaustively search for network architectures though. In practice, we probably don't have the time or computational power to do so. We rarely see researchers searching for the optimal architecture through exhaustive search because the number of choices is so very vast and because there there is more than one correct answer. Instead, we see researchers in this field building onto known architectures through experimentation to attempt to create new novel architectures and improve existing architectures.

So, before we cover strategies for exhaustively searching hyperparameters, let's look at two strategies for deducing a reasonable, even if not the best, network architecture.

Finding a giant and then standing on his shoulders

Bernard of Chartres is attributed with the concept of learning through building on the discoveries of others; however, it was Isaac Newton who said "*If I have seen further, it is by standing on the shoulders of giants.*" To be clear, that's exactly what I'm suggesting here.

If I were going to design a network architecture for a new deep learning problem, the first thing I would do is try to find a similar problem that has been solved before in a satisfactory way. While it might be that no one has solved the problem you're tasked with, something similar likely exists.

There is a very good chance that several possible solutions exist. If that's the case, and if time permits, the average results over a few runs of each might tell you which one works the best. Of course, here we find ourselves quickly slipping into research.

Adding until you overfit, then regularizing

Hopefully, by seeking out architectures for similar problems, you are at least close to an architecture that works for you. What can you do to further optimize your network architecture?

- Across several experimental runs, add layers and/or neurons until your network begins to overfit on the problem. In deep learning speak, add units until you no longer have a high bias model.

- Once you're beginning to overfit, you've found some network architecture that is able to fit the training data very well, and perhaps even too well. At this point, you should focus on reducing variance through the use of dropout, regularization, early stopping, or the like.

This approach is most often attributed to famed neural network researcher Geoffrey Hinton. It's an interesting idea, in that it makes overfitting not something to avoid but rather a good first step in building a network architecture.

While there is no rule that we can use to choose the optimal network architecture, and likely many best architectures exist, I find this strategy to work quite well for me in practice.

Practical advice

If the preceding doesn't feel very scientific to you, I agree. It doesn't to me either, and I don't intend it to be. You most certainly can search for an optimal network architecture between some predefined set of configurations, and that is also a correct approach. In fact, it's arguably more correct as it's more rigorous. This process is intended to be practical advice, to help you get to good enough in as few epochs as possible.

Which hyperparameters should we optimize?

Even if you were to follow my advice above and settle on a good enough architecture, you can and should still attempt to search for ideal hyperparameters within that architecture. Some of the hyperparameters we might want to search include the following:

- Our choice of optimizer. Thus far, I've been using Adam, but an rmsprop optimizer or a well-tuned SGD may do better.
- Each of these optimizers has a set of hyperparameters that we might tune, such as learning rate, momentum, and decay.
- Network weight initialization.
- Neuron activation.
- Regularization parameters such as dropout probability or the regularization parameter used in l2 regularization.
- Batch size.

As implied above, this is not an exhaustive list. There are most certainly more options you could try, including introducing variable numbers of neurons in each hidden layer, varying dropout probability per layer, and so on. The possible combinations of hyperparameters are, as we've been implying, limitless. It is also most certainly possible that these choices are not independent of network architecture, adding and removing layers might result in a new optimal choice for any of these hyperparameters.

Hyperparameter optimization strategies

At this point in the chapter, we've suggested that it is, for the most part, computationally impossible, or at least impractical, to try every single combination of hyperparameters we might want to try. Deep neural networks can certainly take a long time to train. While you can parallelize and throw computational resources at the problem, it's likely that your greatest limiter in searching for hyperparameters will continue to be time.

If time is our greatest constraint, and we can't reasonably explore all possibilities in the time we have, then we will have to create a strategy where we get the most utility in the time we have.

In the remainder of this section, I'll cover some common strategies for hyperparameter optimization and then I'll show you how to optimize hyperparameters in Keras with two of my favorite methods.

Common strategies

There are a common set of strategies for hyperparameter optimization that are used across all machine learning models. At a high level, those strategies include the following:

- Grid search
- Random search
- Bayesian optimization
- Genetic algorithms
- Machine learning for hyperparameters

Grid search is simply the act of trying everything, or at least discrete chunks of everything, and then reporting on the best combination of hyperparameters we've found with brute force. It's guaranteed to find the best solution across the parameter space we've identified, along with every other less good solution.

Grid search isn't very practical for deep learning though. We can't realistically explore every possible value of every possible parameter for all but the most basic of deep neural networks. With **random search**, we randomly sample from each parameter distribution and try *n* of them, where (*n * per example training time*) is the budget of time we're willing to allocate to the problem.

Bayesian optimization methods use previous observations to predict what set of hyperparameters to sample next. While Bayesian optimization methods usually outperform brute force techniques, current research suggests the performance gain over exhaustive methods is somewhat small. Additionally, because Bayesian methods depend on prior experience, they're not embarrassingly parallel by any means.

Genetic algorithms are a very interesting and active area of research for machine learning in general; however, my current opinion is that they are also not a great choice for deep neural network parameter optimization because they again depend on prior experience.

Some of the newest research in this field looks at training neural networks that can predict the best parameters for a given network architecture. The idea of models that can parameterize models is certainly very interesting, and this is a place to watch closely. It also may be how we get Skynet. Only time will tell.

Using random search with scikit-learn

Grid search and random search can be easily implemented with scikit-learn. In this example, we will use the `KerasClassifier` class from Keras to wrap our model and make it compatible with the scikit-learn API. Then, we will use scikit-learn's `RandomSearchCV` class to do the hyperparameter search.

To do this, we will start by changing our now familiar model build function slightly. We will parameterize it with the hyperparameters we would like to search, as shown in the following code:

```
def build_network(keep_prob=0.5, optimizer='adam'):
    inputs = Input(shape=(784,), name="input")
    x = Dense(512, activation='relu', name="hidden1")(inputs)
    x = Dropout(keep_prob)(x)
    x = Dense(256, activation='relu', name="hidden2")(x)
    x = Dropout(keep_prob)(x)
    x = Dense(128, activation='relu', name="hidden3")(x)
    x = Dropout(keep_prob)(x)
    prediction = Dense(10, activation='softmax', name="output")(x)
    model = Model(inputs=inputs, outputs=prediction)
    model.compile(optimizer=optimizer, loss='categorical_crossentropy',
```

```
                    metrics=["accuracy"])
    return model
```

In this example, I would like to search for an ideal value for dropout, and I would like to try several different optimizers. In order to make this happen, I need to include these as parameters in the function so that they can be changed by our random search method. We could, of course, parameterize and test many other network architecture choices using this same methodology, but we're keeping it simple here.

Next, we will create a function that returns a dictionary of all the possible hyperparameters and their value spaces that we'd like to search through, as shown in the following code:

```
def create_hyperparameters():
    batches = [10, 20, 30, 40, 50]
    optimizers = ['rmsprop', 'adam', 'adadelta']
    dropout = np.linspace(0.1, 0.5, 5)
    return {"batch_size": batches, "optimizer": optimizers,
        "keep_prob": dropout}
```

All that's left is to connect these two pieces together using `RandomSearchCV`. First, we will wrap our model into `keras.wrappers.scikit_learn.KerasClassifier` so that it's compatible with scikit-learn, as shown in the following code:

```
model = KerasClassifier(build_fn=build_network, verbose=0)
```

Next, we will get our hyperparameter dictionary, using the following code:

```
hyperparameters = create_hyperparameters()
```

Then, finally, we will create a `RandomSearchCV` object that we will use to search through the parameter space of the model, as shown in the following code:

```
search = RandomizedSearchCV(estimator=model,
param_distributions=hyperparameters, n_iter=10, n_jobs=1, cv=3, verbose=1)
```

Once we fit this `RandomizedSearchCV` object, it will randomly choose values from the parameter distributions and apply them to the model. It will do this 10 times (`n_iter=10`), and it will try each combination three times because we used 3-fold cross-validation. This means we will be fitting the model a total of 30 times. Using the average accuracy across runs, it will return the best model as a class attribute `.best_estimator` and it will return the best parameters as `.best_params_`.

To fit it, we just call its fit method, as if it were a model, as shown in the following code:

```
search.fit(data["train_X"], data["train_y"])

print(search.best_params_)
```

Fitting the MNIST model used in Chapter 5, *Using Keras for Multiclass Classification*, on the above grid takes about 9 minutes on a Tesla K80 GPU instance. Before we call this section done, let's take a look at some of the output for the search, as illustrated in the following code:

```
Using TensorFlow backend.
 Fitting 3 folds for each of 10 candidates, totalling 30 fits
tensorflow/core/common_runtime/gpu/gpu_device.cc:1030] Found device 0 with
properties:
 name: Tesla K80 major: 3 minor: 7 memoryClockRate(GHz): 0.8235
 pciBusID: 0000:00:1e.0
 totalMemory: 11.17GiB freeMemory: 11.10GiB
tensorflow/core/common_runtime/gpu/gpu_device.cc:1120] Creating TensorFlow
device (/device:GPU:0) -> (device: 0, name: Tesla K80, pci bus id:
0000:00:1e.0, compute capability: 3.7)
 [Parallel(n_jobs=1)]: Done 30 out of 30 | elapsed: 8.8min finished
 {'keep_prob': 0.20000000000000001, 'batch_size': 40, 'optimizer': 'adam'}
```

As you can see in this output, across 10 runs it appears that the bolded hyperparameters were the best performing set. Of course we could certainly run for more iterations, and we might find a better option. Our budget is only decided by time, patience, and the credit card attached to our cloud account.

Hyperband

Hyperband is a hyperparameter optimization technique that was developed at Berkley in 2016 by Lisha Li, Kevin Jamieson, Guilia DeSalvo, Afshin Rostamizadeh, and Ameet Talwalker. You can read their original paper at https://arxiv.org/pdf/1603.06560.pdf.

Imagine randomly sampling many potential sets of hyperparameters, as we did above in RandomSearchCV. When RandomSearchCV is done, it will have chosen one single hyperparameter configuration as the *best* among those it sampled. Hyperband exploits the idea that a best hyperparameter configuration is likely to outperform other configurations after even a small number of iterations. The band in Hyperband comes from bandit, referring back to exploration versus exploitation based on multi-arm bandit techniques (techniques used to optimize resource allocation between competing choices with the goal of optimizing performance).

Using Hyperband, we might try some set of possible configurations (*n*), training for only one iteration. The authors leave the term iteration open for multiple possible uses; however, I'll be using epochs as iterations. Once this first loop of training is complete, the resulting configurations are sorted by performance. The top half of this list is then trained for a larger number of iterations. This process of halving and culling is then repeated and we arrive at some very small set of configurations that we will train for full number of iterations we've defined in our search. This process gets us to a *best* set of hyperparameters in a shorter time than searching every possible configuration for max epochs.

In the GitHub repository for this chapter, I've included an implementation of the `hyperband` algorithm, in `hyperband.py`. This implementation is mostly derived from an implementation by FastML, which you can find at `http://fastml.com/tuning-hyperparams-fast-with-hyperband/`. To use it, you need to start by instantiating a `hyperband` object, as shown in the following code:

```
from hyperband import Hyperband
hb = Hyperband(data, get_params, try_params)
```

The Hyperband constructor requires three arguments:

- `data`: The data dictionary that I've been using thus far in the examples
- `get_params`: The name of a function that is used to sample from the hyperparameter space we are searching
- `try_param`: The name of a function that can be used to evaluate a hyperparameter configuration for `n_iter` iterations and return the loss

In the following example, I implement `get_params` to sample in a uniform way across the parameter space:

```
def get_params():
    batches = np.random.choice([5, 10, 100])
    optimizers = np.random.choice(['rmsprop', 'adam', 'adadelta'])
    dropout = np.random.choice(np.linspace(0.1, 0.5, 10))
    return {"batch_size": batches, "optimizer": optimizers,
      "keep_prob": dropout}
```

As you can see, the selected hyperparameter configuration is returned as a dictionary.

Next, `try_params` can be implemented to fit a model for a specified number of iterations on a hyperparameter configuration, as follows:

```
def try_params(data, num_iters, hyperparameters):
    model = build_network(keep_prob=hyperparameters["keep_prob"],
                          optimizer=hyperparameters["optimizer"])
```

```
model.fit(x=data["train_X"], y=data["train_y"],
          batch_size=hyperparameters["batch_size"],
          epochs=int(num_iters))
loss = model.evaluate(x=data["val_X"], y=data["val_y"], verbose=0)
return {"loss": loss}
```

The `try_params` function returns a dictionary that can be used to keep track of any number of metrics; however, loss is required as it's used to compare runs.

The `hyperband` object will run through the algorithm we described above by calling the `.run()` method on it.

```
results = hb.run()
```

In this case`results` will be a dictionary of each run, its runtime, and the hyperparameters tested. Because even this highly optimized search is time-intensive, and because GPU time is expensive, I've included results from the MNIST search in `hyperband-output-mnist.txt` in the GitHub repository for this chapter, which can be found here: `https://github.com/mbernico/deep_learning_quick_reference/tree/master/chapter_6`.

Summary

Hyperparameter optimization is an important step in getting the very best from our deep neural networks. Finding the best way to search for hyperparameters is an open and active area of machine learning research. While you most certainly can apply the state of the art to your own deep learning problem, you will need to weigh the complexity of implementation against the search runtime in your decision.

There are decisions related to network architecture that most certainly can be searched exhaustively, but a set of heuristics and best practices, as I offered above, might get you close enough or even reduce the number of parameters you search.

Ultimately, hyperparameter search is an economics problem, and the first part of any hyperparameter search should be consideration for your budget of computation time, and personal time, in attempting to isolate the best hyperparameter configuration.

This chapter concludes the basics of deep learning. In the next chapter, we will be moving on to some more interesting and advanced applications of neural networks, starting with computer vision.

7
Training a CNN from Scratch

Deep neural networks have revolutionized computer vision. In fact, I'd argue that the advances made in computer vision in just the last few years have made deep neural networks something that many consumers use every day. We've already seen a computer vision classifier in Chapter 5, *Using Keras for Multiclass Classification*, where we used a deep network to classify handwritten digits. Now I want to show you how convolutional layers work, how you can use them, and how you can build your own convolutional neural network in Keras to build better, more powerful deep neural networks to solve computer vision problems.

We will cover the following topics in this chapter:

- Introducing convolutions
- Training a convolutional neural network in Keras
- Using data augmentation

Introducing convolutions

A trained convolutional layer is made up of many feature detectors, called filters, that slide over an input image as a moving window. We will talk about what's inside a filter in a moment, but for now it can be a black box. Imagine a single filter that has already been trained. Maybe that filter has been trained to detect edges in images, which you might think of as transitions between dark and light. As it passes over the image, its output represents the presence and location of the feature it detects, which can be useful for a second layer of filters. Extending our thought experiment slightly further, now imagine a single filter, in a second convolutional layer, that has also already been trained. Perhaps this new layer has learned to detect right angles, where two edges that have been found by the previous layer are present. On and on we go; as we add layers, more intricate features can be learned. This concept of feature hierarchies is central to convolutional neural networks. The following image from *Unsupervised Learning of Hierarchical Representations with Convolutional Deep Belief Networks* by Honglak Lee and others (2011) illustrates the idea of feature hierarchies extremely well:

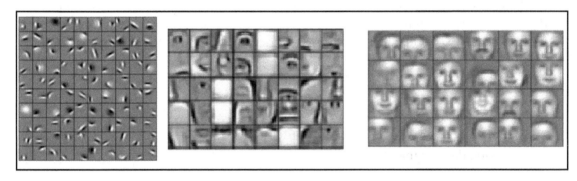

This is a very powerful technique and it possesses several advantages over the `flatten` and `classify` method of deep learning we've previously used on MNIST. We will talk about those shortly, but first let's look deeper inside the filters.

How do convolutional layers work?

In the last section, I said that a convolutional layer is a set of filters that act as feature detectors. Before we move too deep into that architecture, let's review the mathematics of what convolution actually is.

Let's start by manually convolving the following *4 x 4* matrix with a *3 x 3* matrix that we will call a filter. The first step in the convolution process is to take the element wise product of the filter and the first nine boxes of the *4 x 4* matrix:

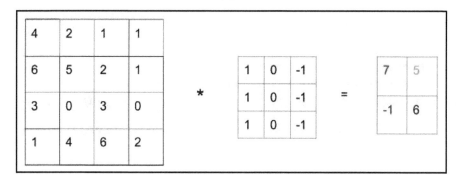

Step 1: 4*1 + 2*0 + 1*-1 + 6*1 + 5*0 + 2*-1 +3*1 + 0*0 + 3 *-1 =

4	2	1	1
6	5	2	1
3	0	3	0
1	4	6	2

*

1	0	-1
1	0	-1
1	0	-1

=

7	

Once we've carried this operation out, we will just slide the filter over one row and do the same thing. Finally, we will slide the filter down, and then over once again. The convolution process, once complete, will leave us with 2x2 matrix, as shown in the following figure:

4	2	1	1
6	5	2	1
3	0	3	0
1	4	6	2

*

1	0	-1
1	0	-1
1	0	-1

=

7	5
-1	6

Technically, this isn't a convolution, but a cross-correlation. We call it a convolution by convention and the difference for our purposes is really quite small.

Convolutions in three dimensions

MNIST was a grayscale example and we could represent each image as a pixel intensity value from 0 to 255, in a two-dimensional matrix. However, most of the time, we will be working with color images. Color images are actually three-dimensional matrices, where the dimensions are the image height, image width, and color. This results in a matrix with separate red, blue, and green values for each pixel in the image.

While we were previously showing two-dimensional filters, we can adapt the idea to three dimensions quite simply by performing the convolution between a (height, width, 3 (colors)) matrix and a *3 x 3 x 3* filter. In the end, we're still left with a two-dimensional output, as we take the elementwise product across all three axes of the matrix. As a reminder, these high-dimension matrices are typically called tensors and what we're doing is making them flow, as it were.

A layer of convolutions

We've previously talked about a layer of a deep neural network consisting of multiple units (which we've been calling neurons) of a linear function, combined with some nonlinearity such as `relu`. In a convolutional layer, each unit is a filter, combined with a nonlinearity. For example, a convolutional layer might be defined in Keras as follows:

```
from keras.layers import Conv2D
Conv2D(64, kernel_size=(3,3), activation="relu", name="conv_1")
```

In this layer, there are 64 separate units, each a *3 x 3 x 3* filter. After the convolution operation is done, each unit adds a bias and a nonlinearity to the output as we did in traditional fully connected layers (more on that term in just a moment).

Before moving on, let's quickly walk through the dimensionality of an example, just so I'm sure we're all on the same page. Imagine we have an input image that is *32 x 32 x 3*. We now convolve it with the above convolutional layer. That layer contains 64 filters, so the output is *30 x 30 x 64*. Each filter outputs a single *30 x 30* matrix.

Benefits of convolutional layers

So, now that you hopefully have an idea how convolutional layers work, let's talk about why we did all this crazy math. Why would we use a convolutional layer instead of the normal layers we have previously been using?

Let's say that we did use a normal layer, to get the same output shape we talked about previously. We started with a *32 x 32 x 3* image, so that's 3,072 values total. We were left with a *30 x 30 x 64* matrix. That's 57,600 values in total. If we were to use a fully connected layer to *connect* these two matrices, that layer would have 176,947,200 trainable parameters. That's 176 million.

However, when we use the convolutional layer above, we used 64 *3 x 3 x 3* filters, which results in 1,728 learnable parameters + 64 biases for a total of 1,792 parameters.

So, obviously a convolutional layer requires much fewer parameters, but why does this matter?

Parameter sharing

Because the filter is used across the entire image, filters learn to detect the features regardless of their position within the image. This turns out to be really useful as it gives us translation invariance, which means we can detect something important regardless of its orientation in the overall image.

Thinking back to MNIST, it's easy to imagine that we might want to detect the loop of a 9, regardless of where it lands in the photo. Thinking ahead, imagine a classifier that classifies pictures as either those of a cat, or a car. It's easy to imagine a set of filters that can detect something as intricate as a car tire. It would be useful to detect that tire regardless of where the car's orientation is in the image, as the presence of something like a tire strongly indicates the image isn't a cat (unless the image is of a cat driving a car).

Local connectivity

Filters focus on connectivity between adjacent pixels, because of their fixed size. This means that they will most strongly learn local features. When combined with other filters in layers, and nonlinearities, this allows us to gradually pay attention to larger and more complex features. This stacking of localized features is really desirable and a key reason why convolutional layers are so great.

Pooling layers

In addition to convolutional layers, convolutional neural networks often use another type of layer called a **pooling layer**. Pooling layers are used to reduce the dimensionality of a convolutional network as layers of convolutions are added, which reduces overfitting. They have the added benefit of making the feature detectors somewhat more robust.

Pooling layers divide a matrix into non-overlapping sections, and then typically take the maximum value (in the case of max pooling) in each region. Alternatively, an average can be employed; however, it is rarely used at this time. The following figure illustrates this technique:

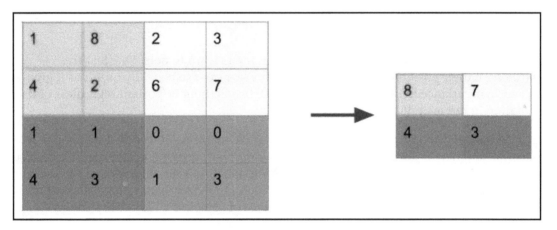

Pooling layers are quite easy to implement in Keras, as we'd expect. The following code can be used for pooling the layers:

```
from keras.layers import MaxPooling2D
pool1 = MaxPooling2D(pool_size=(2, 2), name="pool_1")
```

Here, we're defining the pooling window as *2 x 2*.

While we previously haven't discussed padding, it's common to, in some architectures, pad the input of either a convolutional layer or pooling layer with 0s such that the output dimension is equal to the input. The default in both convolutional and pooling layers in Keras is valid padding, which means no padding by convention. The parameter `padding="same"` will apply padding if you want that.

Batch normalization

Batch normalization helps our networks perform better overall and learn faster. Batch normalization is also fairly easy to understand in an application; however, why it works is still somewhat debated by researchers.

When using batch normalization, for each minibatch, we can normalize that batch to have a mean of 0 and unit variance, after (or before) each nonlinearity. This allows each layer to have a normalized input to learn from, which makes that layer more efficient at learning.

Batch normalization layers are easy to implement in Keras, and I'll be using them after each convolutional layer for the examples in this chapter. The following code is used for batch normalization:

```
from keras.layers import BatchNormalization
x = BatchNormalization(name="batch_norm_1")
```

Training a convolutional neural network in Keras

Now that we've covered the fundamentals of convolutional neural networks, it's time to build one. In this case study, we will be taking on a well-known problem known as **CIFAR-10**. This dataset was created by Alex Krizhevsky, Vinod Nair, and Geoffrey Hinton.

Input

The CIFAR-10 dataset is made up of 60,000 *32 x 32* color images that belong to 10 classes, with 6,000 images per class. I'll be using 50,000 images as a training set, 5,000 images as a validation set, and 5,000 images as a test set.

The input tensor layer for the convolutional neural network will be (N, 32, 32, 3), which we will pass to the `build_network` function as we have previously done. The following code is used to build the network:

```
def build_network(num_gpu=1, input_shape=None):
    inputs = Input(shape=input_shape, name="input")
```

Output

The output of this model will be a class prediction, from 0-9. We will use a 10-node `softmax`, as we did with MNIST. Surprisingly, nothing changes in our output layer. We will use the following code to define the output:

```
output = Dense(10, activation="softmax", name="softmax")(d2)
```

Cost function and metrics

In chapter 5 we used categorical cross-entropy as the loss function for a multiclass classifier. This is just another multiclass classifier and we can continue using categorical cross-entropy as our loss function, and accuracy as a metric. We've moved on to using images as input, but luckily our cost function and metrics remain unchanged.

Convolutional layers

If you were starting to wonder whether there was going to be anything different in this implementation, here it is. I'm going to use two convolutional layers, with batch normalization, and max pooling. This is going to require us to make quite a few choices, which of course we could choose to search as hyperparameters later. It's always better to get something working first though. As Donald Knuth would say, premature optimization is the root of all evil. We will use the following code snippet to define the two convolutional blocks:

```
# convolutional block 1
conv1 = Conv2D(64, kernel_size=(3,3), activation="relu",
name="conv_1")(inputs)
batch1 = BatchNormalization(name="batch_norm_1")(conv1)
pool1 = MaxPooling2D(pool_size=(2, 2), name="pool_1")(batch1)

# convolutional block 2
conv2 = Conv2D(32, kernel_size=(3,3), activation="relu",
```

```
name="conv_2")(pool1)
batch2 = BatchNormalization(name="batch_norm_2")(conv2)
pool2 = MaxPooling2D(pool_size=(2, 2), name="pool_2")(batch2)
```

So, clearly, we have two convolutional blocks here, that consist of a convolutional layer, a batch normalization layer, and a pooling layer.

In the first block, I'm using 64 *3 x 3* filters with `relu` activations. I'm using valid (no) padding and a stride of 1. Batch normalization doesn't require any parameters and it isn't really trainable. The pooling layer is using *2 x 2* pooling windows, valid padding, and a stride of 2 (the dimension of the window).

The second block is very much the same; however, I'm halving the number of filters to 32.

While there are many knobs we could turn in this architecture, the one I would tune first is the kernel size of the convolutions. Kernel size tends to be an important choice. In fact, some modern neural network architectures such as Google's **inception**, allow us to use multiple filter sizes in the same convolutional layer.

Fully connected layers

After two rounds of convolution and pooling, our tensors have gotten relatively small and deep. After `pool_2`, the output dimension is (*n*, 6, 6, 32).

We have, in these convolutional layers, hopefully extracted relevant image features that this *6 x 6 x 32* tensor represents. To classify images, using these features, we will connect this tensor to a few fully connected layers, before we go to our final output layer.

In this example, I'll use a 512-neuron fully connected layer, a 256-neuron fully connected layer, and finally, the 10-neuron output layer. I'll also be using dropout to help prevent overfitting, but only a very little bit! The code for this process is given as follows for your reference:

```
from keras.layers import Flatten, Dense, Dropout
# fully connected layers
flatten = Flatten()(pool2)
fc1 = Dense(512, activation="relu", name="fc1")(flatten)
d1 = Dropout(rate=0.2, name="dropout1")(fc1)
fc2 = Dense(256, activation="relu", name="fc2")(d1)
d2 = Dropout(rate=0.2, name="dropout2")(fc2)
```

I haven't previously mentioned the `flatten` layer above. The `flatten` layer does exactly what its name suggests. It `flattens` the *n x 6 x 6 x 32* tensor into an *n x 1152* vector. This will serve as an input to the fully connected layers.

Multi-GPU models in Keras

Many cloud computing platforms can provision instances that include multiple GPUs. As our models grow in size and complexity you might want to be able to parallelize the workload across multiple GPUs. This can be a somewhat involved process in native TensorFlow, but in Keras, it's just a function call.

Build your model, as normal, as shown in the following code:

```
model = Model(inputs=inputs, outputs=output)
```

Then, we just pass that model to `keras.utils.multi_gpu_model`, with the help of the following code:

```
model = multi_gpu_model(model, num_gpu)
```

In this example, `num_gpu` is the number of GPUs we want to use.

Training

Putting the model together, and incorporating our new cool multi-GPU feature, we come up with the following architecture:

```
def build_network(num_gpu=1, input_shape=None):
    inputs = Input(shape=input_shape, name="input")

    # convolutional block 1
    conv1 = Conv2D(64, kernel_size=(3,3), activation="relu",
      name="conv_1")(inputs)
    batch1 = BatchNormalization(name="batch_norm_1")(conv1)
    pool1 = MaxPooling2D(pool_size=(2, 2), name="pool_1")(batch1)

    # convolutional block 2
    conv2 = Conv2D(32, kernel_size=(3,3), activation="relu",
      name="conv_2")(pool1)
    batch2 = BatchNormalization(name="batch_norm_2")(conv2)
    pool2 = MaxPooling2D(pool_size=(2, 2), name="pool_2")(batch2)

    # fully connected layers
```

```
flatten = Flatten()(pool2)
fc1 = Dense(512, activation="relu", name="fc1")(flatten)
d1 = Dropout(rate=0.2, name="dropout1")(fc1)
fc2 = Dense(256, activation="relu", name="fc2")(d1)
d2 = Dropout(rate=0.2, name="dropout2")(fc2)

# output layer
output = Dense(10, activation="softmax", name="softmax")(d2)

# finalize and compile
model = Model(inputs=inputs, outputs=output)
if num_gpu > 1:
    model = multi_gpu_model(model, num_gpu)
model.compile(optimizer='adam', loss='categorical_crossentropy',
  metrics=["accuracy"])
return model
```

We can use this to build our model:

```
model = build_network(num_gpu=1, input_shape=(IMG_HEIGHT, IMG_WIDTH,
CHANNELS))
```

And then we can fit it, as you'd expect:

```
model.fit(x=data["train_X"], y=data["train_y"],
          batch_size=32,
          epochs=200,
          validation_data=(data["val_X"], data["val_y"]),
          verbose=1,
          callbacks=callbacks)
```

As we train this model, you will notice that overfitting is an immediate concern. Even with a relatively modest two convolutional layers, we're already overfitting a bit.

You can see the effects of overfitting from the following graphs:

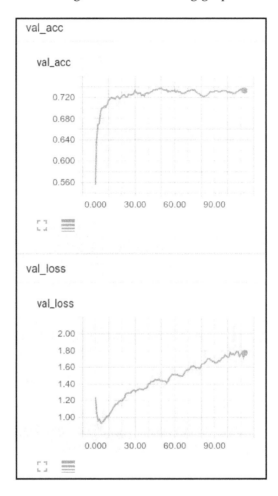

It's no surprise, 50,000 observations is not a lot of data, especially for a computer vision problem. In practice, computer vision problems benefit from very large datasets. In fact, Chen Sun showed that additional data tends to help computer vision models linearly with the log of the data volume in `https://arxiv.org/abs/1707.02968`. Unfortunately, we can't really go find more data in this case. But maybe we can make some. Let's talk about data augmentation next.

Using data augmentation

Data augmentation is a technique where we apply transformations to an image and use both the original image and the transformed images to train on. Imagine we had a training set with a cat in it:

If we were to apply a horizontal flip to this image, we'd get something that looks like this:

This is exactly the same image, of course, but we can use both the original and transformation as training examples. This isn't quite as good as two separate cats in our training set; however, it does allow us to teach the computer that a cat is a cat regardless of the direction it's facing.

In practice, we can do a lot more than just a horizontal flip. We can vertically flip, when it makes sense, shift, and randomly rotate images as well. This allows us to artificially amplify our dataset and make it seem bigger than it is. Of course you can only push this so far, but it's a very powerful tool in the fight against overfitting when little data exists.

The Keras ImageDataGenerator

Not so long ago, the only way to do image augmentation was to code up the transforms and apply them randomly to the training set, saving the transformed images to disk as we went (uphill, both ways, in the snow). Luckily for us, Keras now provides an `ImageDataGenerator` class that can apply transformations on the fly as we train, without having to hand code the transformations.

We can create a data generator object from `ImageDataGenerator` by instantiating it like this:

```
def create_datagen(train_X):
    data_generator = ImageDataGenerator(
        rotation_range=20,
        width_shift_range=0.02,
        height_shift_range=0.02,
        horizontal_flip=True)
    data_generator.fit(train_X)
    return data_generator
```

In this example I'm using both shifts, rotation, and horizontal flips. I'm using only very small shifts. Through experimentation, I found that larger shifts were too much and my network wasn't actually able to learn anything. Your experience will vary as your problem does, but I would expect larger images to be more tolerant of shifting. In this case, we're using 32 pixel images, which are quite small.

Training with a generator

If you haven't used a generator before, it works like an iterator. Every time you call the `ImageDataGenerator.flow()` method, it will produce a new training minibatch, with random transformations applied to the images it was fed.

The Keras Model class comes with a `.fit_generator()` method that allows us to fit with a generator rather than a given dataset:

```
model.fit_generator(data_generator.flow(data["train_X"], data["train_y"],
batch_size=32),
                    steps_per_epoch=len(data["train_X"]) // 32,
                    epochs=200,
                    validation_data=(data["val_X"], data["val_y"]),
                    verbose=1,
                    callbacks=callbacks)
```

Here, we've replaced the traditional x and y parameters with the generator. Most importantly, notice the `steps_per_epoch` parameter. You can sample with replacement any number of times from the training set, and you can apply random transformations each time. This means that we can use more minibatches each epoch than we have data. Here, I'm going to only sample as many batches as I have observations, but that isn't required. We can and should push this number higher if we can.

Before we wrap things up, let's look at how beneficial image augmentation is in this case:

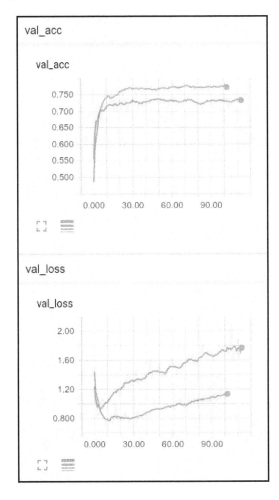

As you can see, just a little bit of image augmentation really helped us out. Not only is our overall accuracy higher, but our network is overfitting much slower. If you have a computer vision problem with just a little bit of data, image augmentation is something you'll want to do.

Summary

In this chapter, we covered a lot of ground fast. We talked about convolutional layers and how they can be used for neural networks. We also covered batch normalization, pooling layers, and data augmentation. Finally, we trained a convolutional neural network from scratch using Keras and then improved that network using data augmentation.

We also talked about how data-hungry computer vision-based deep neural network problems are. In the next chapter I will show you **transfer learning,** which is one of my favorite techniques. It will help solve computer vision problems quickly, with amazing results and much less data.

8
Transfer Learning with Pretrained CNNs

Transfer learning is amazing. In fact, in a book full of amazing things, it might be the most amazing thing I have to tell you about. If not, it's at least perhaps the most useful and pragmatic deep learning technique I can teach you. Transfer learning helps you solve deep learning problems, especially computer vision problems, with very little data and very little computational power relative the problem's scope. In this chapter, we're going to talk about what transfer learning is, when you should use it, and finally how to do transfer learning in Keras.

We will cover the following topics in this chapter:

- Overview of transfer learning
- When transfer learning should be used
- The impact of source/target volume and similarity
- Transfer learning in Keras

Overview of transfer learning

In Chapter 7, *Convolutional Neural Networks*, we trained a convolutional neural network on about 50,000 observations and we saw that, because of the complexity of the network and problem, we were overfitting on the training set after just a few epochs. If you recall, I had made the comment that 50,000 observations in our training set wasn't very large for a computer vision problem. That's true. Computer vision problems love data and the more data we can give them, the better they perform.

The deep neural networks that we might consider state-of-the-art in computer vision are often trained on a dataset called **ImageNet**. The ImageNet dataset (http://www.image-net.org/) is a 1,000 class classifier that contains 1.2 million images. That's more like it! A dataset this large allows researchers the ability to build really complex deep neural networks that can detect sophisticated features. Of course, there's a high price to training a model with sometimes more than 100 layers on 1.2 million images. Training can take weeks and months, not hours.

But what if we could start with one of those state-of-the-art networks, with many layers, trained on millions of images and apply that network to our own computer vision problems, using just a small amount of data? That's **transfer learning**!

To use transfer learning, we will perform the following steps:

1. Start with a model trained on a very big complex computer vision problem; we will call that our source domain
2. Remove the last layer of the network (the softmax layer) and possibly additional fully connected layers
3. Replace those last few layers with layers appropriate for our new problem, which we will call our target domain
4. Freeze all the layers that are already trained so that their weights won't change
5. Train the network on the target domain data

If we stop here, this is most typically called feature extraction because we're using the network trained on the source domain to extract visual features for the target domain. Then we're using a relatively small neural network bolted onto that feature extraction network to perform the target domain task. Depending on our goals and the dataset, this might be enough.

Optionally, we will fine-tune the entire network by unfreezing some or all of the frozen layers and train again, typically with a very small learning rate. We will talk about when to use fine-tuning shortly, but let's make sure we cover some of the reasons to use transfer learning first.

When transfer learning should be used

Transfer learning works really well when you have limited data and when a network exists that solves a similar problem. You can use transfer learning to bring state-of-the art networks and giant volumes of data to an otherwise small problem. So, when should you use transfer learning? Anytime you can! But, there are two stipulations that I'd like you to think about first. We will discuss them in the following sections.

Limited data

The question I'm most often asked when it comes to computer vision and transfer learning is: How many images do I have to have? It's a difficult question to answer because, as we will see in the next section, more is usually better. A better question might be: How few images can I use to solve my business problem adequately?

So, just how limited can our dataset be? While far from scientific, I have built useful models using as few as 2,000 images for binary classification tasks. Simpler tasks and more diverse image sets typically result in more satisfying results with smaller datasets.

As a rule of thumb, you'll need at least a few thousand images of some class, and 10 to 20 thousand images is usually better.

Common problem domains

If your target domain is at least somewhat similar to the source domain, transfer learning tends to work well. For example, imagine you were classifying an image as containing either a cat or a dog. There are many `ImageNet` trained image classifiers that would be ideal to use for this type or problem.

Instead, let's imagine that our problem is to classify a CT scan or MRI as containing a tumor or not. This target domain is very different from the `ImageNet` source domain. As such, while there might be (and probably will be) a benefit in using transfer learning, we will need much more data and probably some fine-tuning to adapt the network to this target domain.

The impact of source/target volume and similarity

Until somewhat recently, there has been very little investigation into the impact that data volume and source/target domain similarity have played in transfer learning performance; however, it's a topic important to the usability of transfer learning and a topic I've written about. In the paper *Investigating the Impact of Data Volume and Domain Similarity on Transfer Learning Applications*, (https://arxiv.org/pdf/1712.04008.pdf), written by my colleagues, Yuntao Li, Dingchao Zhang, and myself, we did some experimentation on these topics. Here's what we found.

More data is always beneficial

In several experiments conducted by Google researchers in the paper *Revisiting Unreasonable Effectiveness of Data in Deep Learning Era,* they constructed an internal dataset that contained 300 million observations, which is obviously much larger than ImageNet. They then trained several state-of-the-art architectures on this dataset, increasing the amount of data shown to the model from 10 million to 30 million, 100 million, and finally 300 million. In doing so, they showed that model performance increased linearly with the log of the number of observations used to train, showing us that more data always helps in the source domain.

But what about the target domain? We repeated the Google experiment using a few datasets that resemble the type we might use during transfer learning, including the Dogs versus Cats dataset that we will use later in this chapter. We found that in the target domain model performance increased linearly with the log of the number of observations used to train, just as it did in the source domain. More data always helps.

Source/target domain similarity

Unique to transfer learning is the concern about how similar your source and target problem domains are to one another. A classifier trained to recognize faces probably won't transfer easily to a target domain recognizing various architectures. We ran experiments where the source and target were as different as possible, as well as experiments where the source and target domain were very similar. Unsurprisingly, when the source and target domains in the transfer learning application are very different they require more data than when they are similar. They also require much more fine-tuning, since the feature extraction layers have a lot of relearning to do, when the domains are visually very different.

Transfer learning in Keras

Unlike in other examples in this book, here we will need to cover both the target domain problem, the source domain problem, and the network architecture we're using. We will start with an overview of the target domain, which is the problem we're trying to solve. Then we will cover the source domain our network was originally trained on and briefly cover the network architecture we will be using. Then, we will spend the rest of the chapter wiring the problem together. We need to consider both domains separately because their size and similarity are closely related to network performance. The closer the target and source are in type, the better the results.

Target domain overview

In this chapter's example, I will be working with Kaggle's `Dogs versus Cats` dataset. This dataset consists of 25,000 images of dogs and cats. It's perfectly balanced between classes at 12,500 each. The dataset can be downloaded from `https://www.kaggle.com/c/dogs-vs-cats/data`.

This is a binary classification problem. Each photograph contains either a dog or a cat, but not both.

This dataset was assembled in 2007 by Jeremy Elson et. al of Microsoft Research, and it's currently hosted at `www.kaggle.com`. It's absolutely free to download and use for academic use, but it does require a Kaggle account and acceptance of their end user license. Just the same, it's a fantastic dataset so I'm including instructions for using it here.

Source domain overview

We will start with a deep neural network trained on ImageNet. If you recall from the *Overview of transfer learning* section, `ImageNet` is a 1,000 class classifier trained on approximately 1.2 million images. Images of both dogs and cats are both present in the `ImageNet` dataset, so our target domain is in fact very similar to our source domain in this case.

Source network architecture

We're going to be using the **Inception-V3** network architecture (`https://www.cv-foundation.org/openaccess/content_cvpr_2016/papers/Szegedy_Rethinking_the_Inception_CVPR_2016_paper.pdf`). The Inception architecture is interesting and quite sophisticated relative to what you've seen so far in this book. If you recall from `Chapter 7`, *Convolutional Neural Networks*, one of the decisions we had to make around our network architecture was a choice in filter size. For each layer, we had to decide if we should use a *3 x 3* filter, for example, instead of a *5 x 5* filter. Of course, maybe another convolution isn't called for at all; it might be that something like pooling might be more appropriate. So, what if we just did all things, at every layer. That's the motivation behind inception.

This architecture is based on a series of modules, or building blocks called **inceptions modules**. In each inception module, the previous activations are given to a *1 x 1* convolution, a *3 x 3* convolution, a *5 x 5* convolution, and a max pooling layer. The output is then concatenated together.

The Inception-V3 network consists of several of these inception modules stacked on top of each other. The final two layers are both fully connected, with the output layer being a 1,000 neuron softmax.

We can load the Inception-V3 network, and it's weights, by using the `InceptionV3` class inside `keras.applications.inception_v3`. Keras has several popular networks available in it's network zoo, all located inside `keras.applications`. It's also possible to load models created in TensorFlow with just a little more work. Converting models trained in other architectures is possible as well, but it's outside the scope of a quick reference.

To load Inception, we just need to instantiate an `InceptionV3` object, which is a Keras model, as shown in the following code:

```
from keras.applications.inception_v3 import InceptionV3
base_model = InceptionV3(weights='imagenet', include_top=False)
```

You may notice, we said `include_top=False` here, which signals that we don't want the top layers of the network. This spares us the work of removing them by hand. When this code runs the first time, it will download the Inception-V3 network architecture and saved weights and cache those for us. Now we just need to add our own fully connected layers.

Transfer network architecture

We will be replacing the final two layers with fully connected layers that are more appropriate for our use case. Since our problem is binary classification, we will replace the output layer with a single neuron with `sigmoid` activation, as shown in the following code:

```
# add a global spatial average pooling layer
x = base_model.output
x = GlobalAveragePooling2D()(x)
# let's add a fully-connected layer
x = Dense(1024, activation='relu')(x)
# and a logistic layer
predictions = Dense(1, activation='sigmoid')(x)

# this is the model we will train
model = Model(inputs=base_model.input, outputs=predictions)
```

Note that we are using a `GlobalAveragePooling2D` layer here. This layer flattens the 4D output of the previous layer into a 2D layer, suitable for our fully connected layer by averaging. It's also possible to accomplish this when you load the base model by specifying `pooling='avg' or 'max'`. It's your call on how you'd like to handle this.

At this point we have a network that is almost ready to train. However, before we do so, we need to remember to freeze the layers in the base model so their weights don't change as the new fully connected layers go crazy trying to learn. To do that, we can just iterate through the layers and set them to be not trainable, using the following code:

```
for layer in base_model.layers:
    layer.trainable = False
```

Data preparation

We will start by downloading the data from Kaggle (`https://www.kaggle.com/c/dogs-vs-cats/data`) and unzipping the `train.zip` in the book's `Chapter08` directory. You'll now have a single directory called `train/` with 25,000 images. Each will be named something like `cat.number.jpg`.

We want to move this data around so that we have separate directories for train, val, and test. Each of these directories should then have a cat and dog directory. This is all very boring and mundane work, so I've created `data_setup.py` to do this for you. Once you run it, the data will all be formatted appropriately for the rest of the chapter.

When you're done, you will have a data directory with the following structure:

```
▼ 📁 data
    ▼ 📁 test
        ▶ 📁 cat
        ▶ 📁 dog
    ▼ 📁 train
        ▶ 📁 cat
        ▶ 📁 dog
    ▼ 📁 val
        ▶ 📁 cat
        ▶ 📁 dog
```

Data input

A quick browse of the images should convince you that you that our images all vary in resolution and size. As you know from Chapter 7, *Convolutional Neural Networks*, however, we will need these images to be a consistent size for our neural network's input tensor. This is a very real-world problem that you'll often face with computer vision tasks. While it's certainly possible to use a program such as **ImageMagick** (http://www.imagemagick.org) to batch resize our images, the Keras ImageDataGenerator class can be used to resize images on the fly, which is what we will do.

Inception-V3 expects 299 x 299 x 3 images. We can specify this target size in the data generators, as shown in the following code:

```
train_datagen = ImageDataGenerator(rescale=1./255)
val_datagen = ImageDataGenerator(rescale=1./255)

train_generator = train_datagen.flow_from_directory(
    train_data_dir,
    target_size=(img_width, img_height),
    batch_size=batch_size,
    class_mode='binary')

validation_generator = val_datagen.flow_from_directory(
    val_data_dir,
```

```
    target_size=(img_width, img_height),
    batch_size=batch_size,
    class_mode='binary')
```

We most certainly could use data augmentation here if we wanted to, but we won't really need it.

Probably the most interesting thing we're doing here is using the data generator's `flow_from_directory()` method. This method takes a path and generates batches of images given that path. It does all the work of lifting the images off the disk for us. Because it does this a batch at a time, we don't even have to keep all 50,000 images in RAM when they aren't needed. Pretty cool, right?

Training (feature extraction)

For this model we're going to train twice. For the first round of training we will do feature extraction for 10 epochs by training with the network frozen, only adjusting the fully connected layer weights, as we discussed in the *Transfer network architecture* section. Then, in the next section we will unfreeze some of the layers and train again, fine-tuning for another 10 epochs, as shown in the following code:

```
data_dir = "data/train/"
val_dir = "data/val/"
epochs = 10
batch_size = 30
model = build_model_feature_extraction()
train_generator, val_generator = setup_data(data_dir, val_dir)
callbacks_fe = create_callbacks(name='feature_extraction')
# stage 1 fit
model.fit_generator(
    train_generator,
    steps_per_epoch=train_generator.n // batch_size,
    epochs=epochs,
    validation_data=val_generator,
    validation_steps=val_generator.n // batch_size,
    callbacks=callbacks_fe,
    verbose=1)

scores = model.evaluate_generator(val_generator, steps=val_generator.n //
batch_size)
print("Step 1 Scores: Loss: " + str(scores[0]) + " Accuracy: " +
str(scores[1]))
```

In the preceding example, we're using the `ImageDataGenerator` *n* attribute to know the total number of images available to the generator and define the steps per epoch as that number divided by the batch size.

The rest of this code should be familiar.

As previously mentioned, we're only going to need to train for about 10 epochs. Now, let's take a look at that training process in TensorBoard:

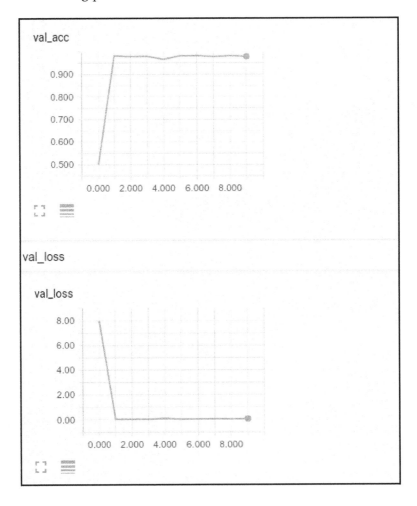

As you can see, the network is performing really well even after a single epoch. We achieve very marginal performance improvements until approximately epoch 7. During epoch 7, we achieve our best performance, resulting in 0.9828 accuracy and 0.0547 loss.

Training (fine-tuning)

In order to fine tune the network, we will need to unfreeze some of those frozen layers. How many layers you unfreeze is your choice and you can unfreeze as much of the network as you like. In practice, most of the time, we only see benefits from unfreezing the top-most layers. Here I'm unfreezing only the very last inception block, which starts at layer 249 on the graph. The following code depicts the this technique:

```
def build_model_fine_tuning(model, learning_rate=0.0001, momentum=0.9):
    for layer in model.layers[:249]:
        layer.trainable = False
    for layer in model.layers[249:]:
        layer.trainable = True
    model.compile(optimizer=SGD(lr=learning_rate,
      momentum=momentum), loss='binary_crossentropy', metrics=
        ['accuracy'])
    return model
```

Also note that I'm using a very small learning rate with **stochastic gradient descent** for fine-tuning. It's important to move weights very slowly at this point to keep from making too big a leap in the wrong direction. I would not recommend using adam or rmsprop for fine-tuning. The following code depicts the fine-tuning mechanism:

```
callbacks_ft = create_callbacks(name='fine_tuning')
# stage 2 fit
model = build_model_fine_tuning(model)
model.fit_generator(
 train_generator,
 steps_per_epoch=train_generator.n // batch_size,
 epochs=epochs,
 validation_data=val_generator,
 validation_steps=val_generator.n // batch_size,
 callbacks=callbacks_ft,
 verbose=2)

scores = model.evaluate_generator(val_generator, steps=val_generator.n //
batch_size)
print("Step 2 Scores: Loss: " + str(scores[0]) + " Accuracy: " +
str(scores[1]))
```

We can review our TensorBoard graphs yet again to see if we get anything with our fine-tuning effort:

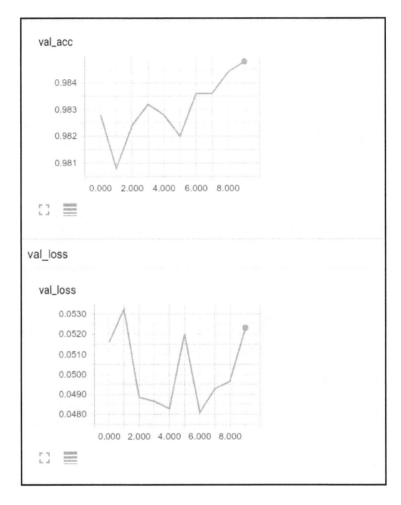

There's no doubt that our model does improve, but only by a very small amount. While the scale is small, you'll notice that the validation loss is struggling to improve and might be showing some signs of beginning to overfit.

In this case, fine-tuning gave little to no benefit, but that isn't always the case. In this example, the target and source domain are very similar. As we learned earlier, as the source and target domain differ, the amount of benefit you get from fine-tuning will increase.

Summary

In this chapter, we covered transfer learning and demonstrated how using a network pre-trained on a source domain can greatly improve the training time, and ultimately the performance of our deep neural network. I hope you enjoy this technique, it's one of my favorites because it's very practical and I typically get great results from it.

In the next chapter, we will move from computer vision to networks that can remember previous inputs, making them ideal for predicting the next item in a sequence.

9
Training an RNN from scratch

Recurrent neural networks (**RNNs**) are a group of neural networks that are built to model sequential data. In the last few chapters, we looked at using convolutional layers to learn features from images. Recurrent layers are equally as useful when we want to learn features from a sequence of values that are all related: x_t, x_{t-1}, x_{t-2}, x_{t-3}.

In this chapter, we will talk about how to use RNNs for time series problems, which are unsurprisingly problems involving a sequence of data points placed in temporal or chronological order.

We will cover the following topics in this chapter:

- Introducing recurrent neural networks
- Time series problems
- Using an LSTM for time series prediction

Introducing recurrent neural networks

In case the definition is unclear, let's look at an example: a stock market ticker where we might observe the price of a stock changing over time, such as Alphabet Inc. in the following screenshot, which is an example of time series:

In the next chapter, we will talk about using recurrent neural networks to model language, which is another type of sequence, a sequence of words. Since you're reading this book, you undoubtedly have some intuition on language sequences already.

If you're new to time series, you might be wondering if it would be possible to use a normal multilayer perceptron to solve a time series problem. You most certainly could do that; however, practically, you almost always get better results using recurrent networks. That said, recurrent neural networks have two other advantages for modeling sequences:

- They can learn really long sequences easier than a normal MLP
- They can handle sequences of varying length

Of course, that leaves us with an important question...

What makes a neuron recurrent?

Recurrent neural networks have loops, which allow information to persist from one prediction to the next. This means that the output for each neuron depends on both the current input, and the previous outputs of the network, as shown in the following image:

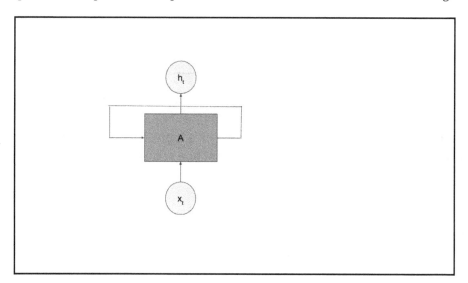

If we were to flatten this diagram out across time, it would look more like the following graph. This idea of the network informing itself is where the term recurrent comes from, although as a CS major I always think of it as a recursive neural network.

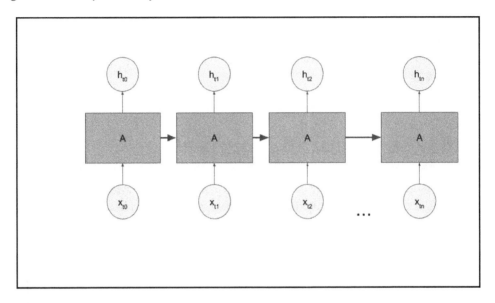

In the preceding diagram, we can see that neuron **A** takes input x_{t0} in and outputs h_{t0} at time step 0. Then at time step 1, the neuron uses input x_{t1}, and a signal from it's previous time step, to output h_{t1}. At time step 2, it now considers it's input x_{t2} and the signal from the previous time step, which may still contain information from time step 0. We continue this way until we reach the final time step in the sequence and the network grows it's memory from step to step.

Standard RNNs use a weight matrix to mix in the previous time step's signal with the product of the current time step's input and the hidden weight matrix. This is all combined before feeding it through a non-linear function, most often a hyperbolic tangent function. For each time step this looks like:

$$a_t = b + W h_{t-1} + U x_t$$

$$h_t = tanh(a_t)$$

$$o_t = c + V h_t$$

Here a_t is a linear combination of the previous time step output and the current time step's input, both parameterized by weight matrices, *W* and *U* respectively. Once a_t has been calculated, it's exposed to a non-linear function, most often the hyperbolic tangent h_t. Finally, the neuron's output o_t combines h_t with a weight matrix, *V*, and *a* bias, *c*.

As you look at this structure, try to imagine a situation where you have some information that's very important, very early in the sequence. As the sequence gets longer, the more likely it is for that important early information to be forgotten as new signals overpower old information easily. Mathematically, the gradient of the unit will either vanish or explode.

This is a major shortcoming of standard RNNs. In practice, traditional RNNs struggle to learn really long-term interactions in a sequence. They're forgetful!

Next, let's take a look at Long Short Term Memory Networks, which can overcome this limitation.

Long Short Term Memory Networks

Long Short Term Memory Networks (**LSTMs**) work really well whenever you might need a recurrent network. As you might have guessed, LSTMs excel at learning long-term interactions. In fact, that's what they were designed to do.

LSTMs are able to both accumulate information from previous time steps, and selectively choose when to forget some irrelevant information in favor of some new more relevant information.

As an example, consider the sequence *In highschool I took Spanish. When I went to France I spoke French.* If we were training a network to predict the word French, it would be very important to remember France and selectively forget Spanish, because the context has shifted. LSTMs can selectively forget things, when the context of the sequence changes.

To accomplish this selective long-term memory, LSTMs implement a forget gate, which earns the LSTM membership into a family of neural networks known as gated neural networks. This forget gate allows the LSTM to selectively learn when information should be discarded from it's long term memory.

Another key characteristic of the LSTM is an internal self loop, that lets the unit accumulate information for long terms. This loop is used in addition to the loop we've seen in the RNN, which can be thought of as an outer loop between time steps.

Relative to the other neurons we've seen, LSTMs are quite complex, as shown in the following image:

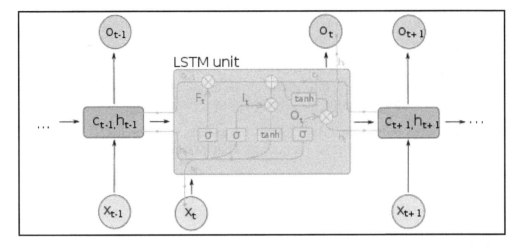

Each LSTM unit, when unrolled, has an input for time step t called x_t, an output called o_t, and a memory bus C that carries memory from the previous time step C_{t-1} to the next C_t.

In addition to these inputs, the unit also contains several gates. The first, which we've already mentioned, is the forget gate, labeled F_t in the diagram:

$$F_t = \sigma(W_f \cdot [h_{t-1}, x_t] + b_f)$$

The output of this gate, which will be between 0 and 1, is pointwise multiplied with C_{t-1}. This allows the gate to regulate the flow of information from C_{t-1} to C_t.

The next gate, the input gate i_t, is used in conjunction with a function Candidate C_t. Candidate C_t learns a vector that could be added to the memory state. The input gate learns which values in the bus C get updated. The following formula illustrates i_t and Candidate C_t:

$$i_t = \sigma(W_i \cdot [h_{t-1}, x_t] + b_i)$$

$$CandidateC_t = tanh(W_C \cdot [h_{t-1}, x_t] + b_C$$

We take the pointwise product of i_t and Candidate C_t decides what to add to bus C, after using F_t to decide what to forget, as shown in the following formula:

$$C_t = F_t \otimes C_{t-1} + i_t \otimes CandidateC_t$$

Finally, we will decide what gets output. The output comes primarily from the memory bus C; however, it's filtered by yet another gate called the output gate. The following formula illustrates the output:

$$OutGate = \sigma(W_o \cdot [h_{t-1}, x_t] + b_o)$$

$$o_t = OutGate \otimes tanh(C_t)$$

While complex, LSTMs are incredibly effective at a variety of problems. While multiple variants of the LSTM exist, this basic implementation is for the most part still considered state-of-the-art across a very wide range of tasks.

One of those tasks is predicting the next value in a time series, which is what we will be using an LSTM for in this chapter. However, before we start applying LSTMs to a time series, a brief refresher on time series analysis and more traditional methods is warranted.

Backpropagation through time

Training an RNN requires a slightly different implementation of **backpropagation**, known as **backpropagation through time (BPTT)**.

As with normal backpropagation, the goal of BPTT is to use the overall network error to adjust the weights of each neuron/unit with respect to their contribution to the overall error, by the gradient. The overall goal is the same.

When using BPTT, our definition of error slightly changes however. As we just saw, a recurrent neuron can be unrolled through several time steps. We care about the prediction quality at all of those time steps, not just the terminal time step, because the goal of an RNN is to predict a sequence correctly, given that a logic unit error is defined as the sum of the error across all unrolled time steps.

When using BPTT, we need to sum up the error across all time steps. Then, after we've computed that overall error, we will adjust the unit's weights by the gradients for each time step.

This forces us to explicitly define how far we will unroll our LSTM. You'll see this in the following example, when we create a specific set of time steps what we will train on for each observation.

The number of steps you choose to backpropagate across is of course a hyperparameter. If you need to learn something from very far back in the sequence, obviously you'll have to include that many lags in the series. You'll need to be able to capture the relevant period. On the other hand, capturing too many time steps also isn't desirable. The network will become very hard to train because, as the gradient propagates through time, it will become very small. This is another instantiation of the vanishing gradient problem that I've described in previous chapters.

As you imagine this scenario, you might wonder if choosing too large of a time step will crash your program. If our gradients are driven so small that they become NaN then we can't complete the update operation. A common and easy way to handle this issue is to fix the gradient between some upper and lower threshold, which we call gradient clipping. All **Keras** optimizers have gradient clipping turned on by default. If your gradient is clipped, the network probably won't learn much for that time step, but at least your program won't crash.

If BPTT seems really confusing, just imagine the LSTM in it's unrolled state, where a unit exists for each time step. For that network structure, the algorithm is really pretty much identical to standard backpropagation, with the exception that all the unrolled layers share weights.

A refresher on time series problems

Time series problems are problems involving a sequence of data points placed in temporal order. We most often represent those data points as a set:

$$X = \left[x_t, x_{t-1}, x_{t-2}, x_{t-3} \ldots x_{t-n} \right]$$

Usually our goal in time series analysis is forecasting; however, there are certainly many other interesting things you can do with a time series that are outside the scope of this book. Forecasting is really just a specialized form of regression, where our goal is to predict some point x_t or points $x_t, x_{t+1}, x_{t+2}, \ldots x_{t+n}$, given some set of previous points $x_{t-1}, x_{t-2}, \ldots x_{t-n}$. We can do this when the time series is auto correlated, which means the data points are correlated with themselves one or more points back in time (which are called lags). The stronger the auto correlation, the easier it is to forecast.

In many books, time series problems are denoted with y, rather than x, as a hint towards the idea that we typically care to predict a variable y given itself.

Stock and flow

In econometric time series, quantities are often defined as **stock** or **flow**. A stock measurement refers to a quantity at a specific point in time. For example, the value of the S and P 500 on December 31, 2008 is a stock measurement. A flow measurement is a rate over an interval of time. The rate the US Stock Market increased from 2009 to 2010 is a flow measurement.

Most often when forecasting, we care to forecast flow. If we imagine forecasting as a specific kind of regression then the first and most obvious reason for our preference for flow is because flow estimates are far more likely to be interpolation instead of extrapolation, and interpolation is almost always safer. Additionally, most time series models have an assumption of stationarity. A stationary time series is one whose statistical properties (mean, variance, and autocorrelation) that are constant over time. If we were to use stock measurements of a quantity, we would find that most real-world problems would be far from stationary.

While there aren't assumptions (read rules) requiring stationarity when using LSTMs for time series analysis, in practical experience, I've found LSTMs trained on relatively stationary data to be far more robust. First order differencing is sufficient in almost all cases when using LSTMs for time series forecasting.

Converting a stock quantity to a flow quantity is fairly straightforward. If you have n points, you can create n-1 flow measurements with first-order differencing, where, for each value t'_n, we calculate it by subtracting t_{n-1} from t_n, giving us the rate of change between the measurements across the interval, as shown in the following formula:

$$t\prime_n = t_n - t_{n-1}$$

For example, if we owned a stock in March worth 80 dollars, and it were suddenly worth 100 dollars in April, the flow rate of the quantity would be 20 dollars.

First-order differencing doesn't guarantee a stationary time series. We might also need to remove seasons or trends. De-trending is a big part of the daily life of professional forecasters. If we were using a traditional statistical model to forecast, more work would be required. While we don't have the pages to cover that, we may also need to perform second order differencing, seasonal detrending, or more. The **augmented Dickey-Fuller** (**ADF**) test is a statistical test often used to determine if our time series is in fact stationary. If you'd like to know if your time series is stationary, you can used the augmented Dickey-Fuller test to check (`https://en.wikipedia.org/wiki/Augmented_Dickey%E2%80%93Fuller_test`). For LSTMs, however, first-order differencing might often be good enough; just understand that the network most certainly will learn seasons and periods left in your dataset.

ARIMA and ARIMAX forecasting

The family of **Auto Regressive Integrated Moving Average** (**ARIMA**) models are worth mentioning because they are traditionally used in time series forecasting. While I'm obviously a big fan of deep neural networks (in fact I wrote a book about them), I suggest starting with ARIMA and progressing towards deep learning. In many cases, ARIMA will outperform the LSTM. This is especially true when data is sparse.

Start with the simplest model that could possibly work. Sometimes that will be a deep neural network, but often it will be something much simpler, such as a linear regression or an ARIMA model. The model's complexity should be justified by the lift it provides, and often simpler is better. While reiterated several times throughout the book, this statement is more true in time series prediction than perhaps any other topic.

The ARIMA model is a combination of three parts. The AR, or autoregressive part, is the part that seeks to model the series based on it's own autocorrelation. The MA portion attempts to model local surprises or shocks in the time series. The I portion covers differencing, which we've just covered. The ARIMA model typically takes three hyperparameters, p, d, and q, which correspond to the number of autoregressive lags modeled, the degree of differencing, and the order of the moving average portion of the model, respectively.

The ARIMA model is very well implemented in R's `auto.arima()` and forecast packages, which is probably one of the only good reasons to use the R language.

The ARIMAX model allows for the inclusion of one or more covariates in the time series model. What's a covariate in this case, you ask? It's an additional time series that is also correlated to the dependent variable and can be used to further improve the performance of forecasting.

A common practice amongst traders is to attempt to predict the value of some commodity by using one or more lags from another commodity as well as autoregressive portions of the commodity we're forecasting. This is a case where the ARIMAX model would be useful.

If you have many covariates with intricate higher order interactions, you've landed in the sweet spot of LSTM for time series prediction. At the beginning of the book, we talked about how a multilayer perceptron can model complicated interactions between input variables giving us automatic feature engineering that provides lift over a linear or logistic regression. This property is carried forward to using LSTMs for time series prediction with many input variables.

If you'd like to learn more about ARIMA, ARIMAX, and time series forecasting in general, I recommend starting with Rob J. Hyndman's blog Hyndsight at `https://robjhyndman.com/hyndsight/`.

Using an LSTM for time series prediction

In this chapter, we're going to predict the minute-to-minute value of bitcoin in US dollars during the month of June 2017 by using the minute-to-minute price of bitcoin from January to May of 2017. I know this sounds really lucrative but before you buy that boat, I recommend reading through to the end of the chapter; this is something easier said and even easier modeled, than done.

Even if we were able to create the potential for an arbitrage (a difference in price between two markets due to an inefficiency) between USD and bitcoins using some model like this one, developing a trading strategy around bitcoin can be extremely complex because of the delay in finalizing bitcoin transactions. At the time of this writing, the average transaction time for a bitcoin transaction is over an hour! This "illiquidity" should be a consideration in any trading strategy.

As before, the code for this chapter is available in the book's Git repository under `Chapter09`. The file `data/bitcoin.csv` contains several years worth of bitcoin prices. We will only be using a few months of price information for our model, based on the hypothesis that the market behavior in prior years wasn't relevant to the behavior of 2017, when the cryptocurrency became popular.

Data preparation

For this example, we won't be using a validation set, or rather we will be using our test set as our validation set. When working on forecasting problems like this one, validation becomes a challenging endeavor because the further the training data gets from the testing data, the more likely it is to perform poorly. On the other hand, this doesn't provide much protection from overfitting.

To keep things simple, here we will use only a test set and hope for the best.

Before we move on, let's take a look at the overall flow for the data prep we will do. In order to use this dataset to train an LSTM, we will need to:

1. Load the dataset and convert epoch times into pandas date times.
2. Create a train and test set by slicing on date ranges.
3. Difference our dataset.
4. Scale the differences to be in a scale closer to our activation functions. We will use -1 to 1 since we're going to be using `tanh` as the activation
5. Create a training set where each target x_t has a sequence of lags $x_{t-1}...x_{t-n}$ associated with it. In this training set, you can think of x_t as our typical dependent variable y. The sequence of lags $x_{t-1}...x_{t-n}$ can be thought of as the typical X training matrix.

I'm going to cover each step in the coming topics, showing the relevant code as we go.

Loading the dataset

Loading our dataset from disk is a fairly straightforward endeavor. As we previously mentioned, we will be slicing our data by date. To do this, we will need to convert the Unix epoch times in the dataset to more sliceable dates. This is easily accomplished with the pandas to_datetime() method, as shown in the following code:

```
def read_data():
    df = pd.read_csv("./data/bitcoin.csv")
    df["Time"] = pd.to_datetime(df.Timestamp, unit='s')
    df.index = df.Time
    df = df.drop(["Time", "Timestamp"], axis=1)
    return df
```

Slicing train and test by date

We can construct a date-based slicing function now that our dataframe is indexed by a datetime timestamp. To do so, we will define a Boolean mask and use that mask to select the existing dataframe. While we could certainly construct this in one line, I think it's a little easier to read this way, as shown in the following code:

```
def select_dates(df, start, end):
    mask = (df.index > start) & (df.index <= end)
    return df[mask]
```

Now that we can grab portions of the dataframe using dates, we can easily create a training and test dataframe with a few calls to these functions, using the following code:

```
df = read_data()
df_train = select_dates(df, start="2017-01-01", end="2017-05-31")
df_test = select_dates(df, start="2017-06-01", end="2017-06-30")
```

Before we can use these datasets, we will need to difference them, as shown next.

Differencing a time series

Pandas dataframes were originally created to operate on time series data, and luckily for us, because differencing a dataset is such a common operation in time series, it's conveniently built in. As a matter of good coding practice, however, we will wrap a function around our first-order differencing operation. Note that we will be filling any spaces where we couldn't do first- order differencing with 0. The following code illustrates this technique:

```
def diff_data(df):
    df_diffed = df.diff()
    df_diffed.fillna(0, inplace=True)
    return df_diffed
```

By differencing the dataset, we've moved this problem, a stock problem, to a flow problem. In the cast of bitcoin, the flow can be quite large because the value of a bitcoin can change a great deal between minutes. We will address this by scaling the dataset.

Scaling a time series

We will use `MinMaxScaler` in this example to scale each difference data point into a scale with a minimum value of -1 and a maximum value of 1. This will put our data on the same scale as the hyperbolic tangent function (`tanh`), which is our activation function for the problem. We will use the following code for scaling the series:

```
def scale_data(df, scaler=None):
    scaled_df = pd.DataFrame(index=df.index)
    if not scaler:
        scaler = MinMaxScaler(feature_range=(-1,1))
    scaled_df["Price"] =
scaler.fit_transform(df.Close.values.reshape(-1,1))
    return scaler, scaled_df
```

Note that this function can optionally take a scaler that's already been fit. This allows us to apply our train scalers on our test set.

Creating a lagged training set

For each training example, we want to train the network to predict a value x_t, given a sequence of lags $xt - 1...xt - n$. The ideal number of lags is a hyperparameter, so some experimentation is in order.

Structuring the input in this way is a requirement of the BPTT algorithm, as we have previously talked about. We will use the following code to train the dataset:

```
def lag_dataframe(data, lags=1):
    df = pd.DataFrame(data)
    columns = [df.shift(i) for i in range(lags, 0, -1)]
    columns.append(df)
    df = pd.concat(columns, axis=1)
    df.fillna(0, inplace=True)

    cols = df.columns.tolist()
    for i, col in enumerate(cols):
        if i == 0:
            cols[i] = "x"
        else:
            cols[i] = "x-" + str(i)

    cols[-1] = "y"
    df.columns = cols
    return df
```

As an example, if we were to call `lag_dataframe` with `lags` = 3, we would expect a dataset returned with x_{t-1}, x_{t-2}, and x_{t-3}. I find it very difficult to understand lag code like this, so if you do too, you aren't alone. I recommend running it and building some familiarity with the operation.

> When choosing the number lags, you might need to also consider how many lags you want to wait for before you're able to make a prediction, when you deploy your model to production.

Input shape

Keras expects the input for our LSTM to be a three-dimensional tensor that looks like:

$$Samples * Sequence\ Length(Timesteps) * Features\ per\ Timestep$$

The first dimension is obviously the number of observations we have, and we would expect that.

The second dimension corresponds to the number of lags we've chosen when using the `lag_dataframe` function. This is the number of time steps we're going to give Keras in order to make a prediction.

The third dimension is the number of features present in that time step. In our example, we'll be using one, because we only have one feature per time step, that time step's bitcoin price.

Before reading on, consider carefully the power that defining a three dimensional matrix here gives you. We absolutely could include hundreds of other time series as features to predict this time series. In doing so, and in using an LSTM, we get feature engineering between those features for free. It's this functionality that makes LSTMs so exciting in the financial domains.

For the problem at hand, we will need to convert our two-dimensional matrix into a three-dimensional matrix. To do so we will use NumPy's handy `reshape` function, as shown in the following code:

```
X_train = np.reshape(X_train.values, (X_train.shape[0], X_train.shape[1],
1))
X_test = np.reshape(X_test.values, (X_test.shape[0], X_test.shape[1], 1))
```

Data preparation glue

We've done a lot of transformation in this example. Before moving on to training, I think it might be a good idea to see how this all fits together. We will use one more function, as shown here, to tie all these steps together:

```
def prep_data(df_train, df_test, lags):
    df_train = diff_data(df_train)
    scaler, df_train = scale_data(df_train)
    df_test = diff_data(df_test)
    scaler, df_test = scale_data(df_test, scaler)
    df_train = lag_dataframe(df_train, lags=lags)
    df_test = lag_dataframe(df_test, lags=lags)

    X_train = df_train.drop("y", axis=1)
    y_train = df_train.y
    X_test = df_test.drop("y", axis=1)
    y_test = df_test.y

    X_train = np.reshape(X_train.values, (X_train.shape[0],
X_train.shape[1], 1))
```

```
    X_test = np.reshape(X_test.values, (X_test.shape[0], X_test.shape[1],
1))

    return X_train, X_test, y_train, y_test
```

This function takes our train and test dataframes and applies differencing, scaling, and lagging code. It then realigns those dataframes into our familiar *X* and *y* tensors for both train and test.

We can now get from loading the data to being ready to train and test with just a few lines of code that glue these transformations together:

```
LAGS=10
df = read_data()
df_train = select_dates(df, start="2017-01-01", end="2017-05-31")
df_test = select_dates(df, start="2017-06-01", end="2017-06-30")
X_train, X_test, y_train, y_test = prep_data(df_train, df_test, lags=LAGS)
```

And with that we're ready to train.

Network output

Our network will be outputting a single value, which is the scaled flow or expected change of the bitcoin price in some given minute based on the previous minutes.

We can get this output by using a single neuron. This neuron can be implemented in a Keras Dense Layer. It will take, as inputs, the output of multiple LSTM neurons, which we will cover in the next section. Lastly, the activation of this neuron can be `tanh` because we've scaled our data to the same scale as the hyperbolic tangent function, as seen here:

```
output = Dense(1, activation='tanh', name='output')(lstm2)
```

Network architecture

Our network will use two Keras LSTM layers, each with 100 LSTM units:

```
inputs = Input(batch_shape=(batch_shape, sequence_length,
            input_dim), name="input")
lstm1 = LSTM(100, activation='tanh', return_sequences=True,
         stateful=True, name='lstm1')(inputs)
lstm2 = LSTM(100, activation='tanh', return_sequences=False,
         stateful=True, name='lstm2')(lstm1)
output = Dense(1, activation='tanh', name='output')(lstm2)
```

Pay special attention to the `return_sequences` argument. When connecting two LSTM layers, you need the previous LSTM layer to output predictions for each time step in the sequence so that the input for the next LSTM layer is three-dimensional. Our Dense layer, however, only needs a two-dimensional output in order to predict the exact time step it's tasked with predicting.

Stateful versus stateless LSTMs

Earlier in the chapter, we talked about an RNN's ability to maintain state, or memory, across time steps.

When using Keras, LSTMs can be configured in two ways, **stateful** and **stateless**.

The stateless configuration is the default. When you use a stateless LSTM configuration, LSTM cell memory is reset every batch. This makes batch size a very important consideration. Stateless works best when the the sequences you're learning aren't dependent on one another. Sentence-level prediction of a next word might be a good example of when to use stateless.

The stateful configuration resets LSTM cell memory every epoch. This configuration is most commonly used when each sequence in the training set depends on the sequence that comes before it. If sentence-level prediction might be a good task for a stateless configuration, document-level prediction might be a good task for a stateful model.

Ultimately, this choice is dependent on the problem and may require some experimentation where each option is tested.

For this example, I've tested each option and have chosen to use a stateful model. That's probably not surprising when we consider the context of the problem.

Training

While things might seem very different at this point, training an LSTM is actually not any different than training a deep neural network on a typical cross-sectional problem:

```
LAGS=10
df = read_data()
df_train = select_dates(df, start="2017-01-01", end="2017-05-31")
df_test = select_dates(df, start="2017-06-01", end="2017-06-30")
X_train, X_test, y_train, y_test = prep_data(df_train, df_test, lags=LAGS)
model = build_network(sequence_length=LAGS)
```

```
callbacks = create_callbacks("lstm_100_100")
model.fit(x=X_train, y=y_train,
          batch_size=100,
          epochs=10,
          callbacks=callbacks)
model.save("lstm_model.h5")
```

After preparing our data, we instantiate a network with the architecture we've walked through and then call fit on it as expected.

Here I'm using a stateful LSTM. One practical benefit of stateful LSTMs is that they tend to train in fewer epochs than stateless LSTMs. If you were to refactor this as a stateless LSTM, you might need 100 epochs before the network has finished learning, whereas here we are only using 10.

Measuring performance

After 10 epochs in a stateful configuration, our loss has stopped improving and our network is fairly well trained, as you can see from the following graph:

We have a fit network that appears to have learned something. We can now make some sort of prediction as to the price flow of bitcoin. If we're able to do it well, we will all be very rich. Before we go buy that mansion, we should probably measure our model's performance.

The ultimate test of a financial model is this question: *Are you willing to put money on it?* It's difficult to answer this question because measuring performance in a time series problem can be challenging.

One very simple way to measure performance would be to use a root mean squared error to evaluate the difference between `y_test` and a prediction on `X_test`. We most certainly could do that, as shown in the following code:

```
RMSE = 0.0801932157201
```

Is 0.08 a good score? Let's start our investigation into good by comparing our predictions, against the actual values for bitcoin flow in June. Doing so might give us some visual intuition behind the the model's performance and is a practice I always recommend:

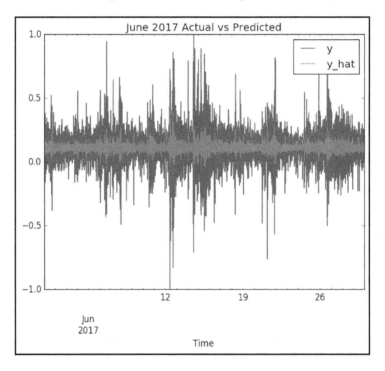

Our predictions, in green, leave quite a bit to be desired. Our model has learned to predict average flow, but it's really doing a very poor job at matching the full signal. It's even possible we might just be learning a trend, because of our less than vigorous detrending we did. I think we might have to put that mansion off a bit longer, but we're on the right path.

Consider our prediction as the model explaining as much of the price of bitcoin as possible, given only the previous value of bitcoin. We are probably doing a fairly good job of modeling the autoregressive parts of the time series. But, there are likely many different external factors that impact the price of bitcoin. The value of the dollar, the movement of other markets, and perhaps, most importantly, the buzz or information flow around bitcoin, are all likely play an important role in it's price.

And that's where the power of LSTMs for time series prediction really come into play. By adding additional input features, all of this information can be somewhat easily added to the model, hopefully explaining more and more of the entire picture.

But, let me dash your hopes one more time. A more thorough investigation on performance would also include consideration for the lift the model provides over some naive model. Typical choices for this simple model might include something called a **random walk** model, an exponential smoothing model, or possibly by using a naive approach such as using the previous time step as the prediction for the current time step. This is illustrated in the following graph:

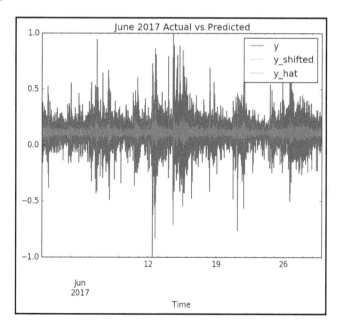

In this graph, we're comparing our predictions in red, to a model where we're just using the previous minute as the prediction for the next minute, in green. In blue, the actual price, overlays this naive model almost perfectly. Our LSTM prediction isn't nearly as good as the naive model. We would be better off by just using the last minute's price to predict the current minute's price. While I stand by the assertion that we're on the right track, we have a long way to go before that boat is ours.

Modeling any commodity is very difficult. Using a deep neural networks for this type of problem is promising to be sure, but the problem is not an easy one. I'm including this perhaps exhaustive explanation so that if you decide to head down this path, you understand what you're in for.

That said, when you do use an LSTM to arbitrage a financial market, please remember to tip your author.

Summary

In this chapter, we talked about using recurrent neural networks to predict the next element in a sequence. We covered both RNNs in general and LSTMs specifically, and we focused on using LSTMs to predict a time series. In order to make sure we understood the benefits and challenges of using LSTMs for time series, we briefly reviewed some basics of time series analysis. We spent a few minutes talking about traditional time series models as well, including ARIMA and ARIMAX.

Lastly, we walked through a challenging use case where we used an LSTM to predict the price of a bitcoin.

In the next chapter, we will continue to use RNNs, now focusing on natural language processing tasks and introducing the concept of embedding layers.

10
Training LSTMs with Word Embeddings from Scratch

So far, we've seen examples of the application of deep learning in structured data, image data, and even time series data. It seems only right to move on to **natural language processing** (**NLP**) as the next stop on our tour. The connection between machine learning and human language is a fascinating one. Deep learning has exponentially accelerated the pace at which this field is moving, as it has with computer vision. Let's start with a brief overview of NLP and some of the tasks we'll be taking on in this chapter.

We will also cover the following topics in this chapter:

- An introduction to natural language processing
- Vectorizing text
- Word embedding
- Keras embedding layer
- 1D CNNs for natural language processing
- Case studies for document classifications

An introduction to natural language processing

The field of NLP is vast and complex. Any interaction between human language and computer science might technically fall into this category. For the sake of this discussion though, I'll confine NLP to analyzing, understanding, and, sometimes, generating human language.

From the beginnings of computer science, we've been fascinated by NLP as a gateway to strong artificial intelligence. In 1950, Alan Turing proposed the Turing test, which involves a computer impersonating a human so well that it's indistinguishable from another human, as a metric for machine intelligence. Ever since, we've worked to find clever ways to help machines understand human language. Along the way, we've developed speech-to-text transcription, automatic translation between human languages, the automatic summation of documents, topic modeling, named entity identification, and a variety of other use cases.

As our understanding of NLP continues to grow, we find AI applications becoming common in everyday life. Chatbots have become commonplace as customer service applications and, more recently, they have become our personal digital assistants. As I write this, I'm able to ask Alexa to add something to my shopping list or play some smooth jazz. Natural language processing connects humans to computers in a very interesting and powerful way.

In this chapter, I'm going to focus on understanding human language and then using that understanding to classify. I will actually have two classification case studies, one that covers semantic analysis and another that covers document classification. Both case studies provide great opportunities for the application of deep learning, and they're really very similar.

Semantic analysis

Semantic analysis is technically the analysis of the meaning of language, but usually when we say semantic analysis, we are talking about understanding the feelings of the author. Semantic classifiers are typically trying to classify some utterance as positive, negative, happy, sad, neutral, and so on.

One of my favorite features of human language, sarcasm, makes this a challenging problem to solve. There are many subtle patterns in human language that are very challenging for computers to learn. But challenging doesn't mean impossible. Given a good dataset, this task is very possible.

Success for this type of problem requires a good dataset. While we can most certainly find ample amounts of human conversation all over the internet, most of it isn't labeled. Finding labeled cases is more challenging. An early attempt at solving this problem was to gather twitter data that contained emoticons. If a tweet contained a :), it was considered a positive tweet. This became the well-named emoticon trick referenced in `Large-Scale Machine Learning at Twitter` by Jimmy Lin and Alek Kolcz.

Most business applications of this type of classifier are binary, where we attempt to predict if the customer is happy or not. That's certainly not the limit to this type of language model, however. We can model other tones as long as we have labels for that sort of thing. We might even attempt to measure anxiety or distress in someone's voice or language; however, addressing audio input is outside the scope of this chapter.

Further attempts to mine data have included using the language associated with positive and negative movie reviews and language related to online shopping product reviews. These are all great approaches; however, great care should be used when using these types of data sources to classify text from a different domain. As you might imagine, the language used in a movie review or an online purchase might be very different from the language used in an IT helpdesk customer support call.

Of course, we can certainly classify more than just sentiment. We will talk about the more general application of document classification in the following section.

Document classification

Document classification is closely related to sentiment analysis. In both cases, we're classifying documents into categories using their text. It's really only the why that changes. Document classification is all about classifying a document based on its type. The world's most obvious and common document classification system is a spam filter, but that has many other uses.

One of my favorite uses of document classification is in settling the debate around the original authors of *The Federalist Papers*. Alexander Hamilton, James Madison, and John Jay published 85 essays under the pseudonym Publius in 1787 and 1788 supporting the ratification of the United States Constitution. Later, Hamilton provided a list detailing the author of each paper before his fatal duel with Aaron Burr in 1804. Madison provided his own list in 1818 that created a dispute in authorship that scholars have been attempting to solve ever since. While it's mostly agreed upon that the disputed works belonged to Madison, there remain some theories as to a collaborative effort between the two. Classifying these 12 disputed documents as either Madison or Hamilton has been fodder for many a data science blog. Most formally, the paper, `The Disputed Federalist Papers: SVM Feature Selection via Concave Minimization`, by Glenn Fung covers the topic with quite a bit of rigor.

A final example of document classification might be around understanding the content of the document and prescribing action. Imagine a classifier that might read some information about a legal case, for example, the petition/complaint and summons, and then make a recommendation to the defendant. Our imaginary system might then say, *given my experience with other cases like this one, you probably want to settle*.

Sentiment analysis and documentation classification are powerful techniques based on the computer's ability to understand natural language. But, of course, this begs the question, how do we teach computers to read?

Vectorizing text

Machine learning models, including deep neural networks, take numeric information in and produce numeric output. The challenge with natural language processing then becomes, naturally, converting words to numbers.

There are a variety of ways that we can convert words to numbers. All of these methods satisfy the same goal, converting some sequence of words into a numeric vector. Some methods work better than others because, sometimes, when we make this conversion, we can lose some meaning in the translation.

NLP terminology

Let's start with by defining a few common terms, so that we remove any ambiguity their use might cause. I know that, since you can read, you likely have some understanding of these terms. I apologize if this seems pedantic, but I do promise it will immediately relate to the models we talk about next:

- **Words**: The atomic element of most of the systems we will be using. While some character level models do exist, we won't be talking about them today.
- **Sentence**: A collection of words that expresses a statement, question, and so on.
- **Document**: A document is a collection of sentences. It might be a sentence, or more likely multiple sentences.
- **Corpus**: A collection of documents.

Bag of Word models

The **Bag of Word** (**BoW**) models are NLP models that really disregard sentence structure and word placement. In a Bag of Word model, we treat each document as a bag of words. It's easy to imagine just that. Each document is a container that holds a big set of words. We ignore sentences, structure, and which words come first or last. We concern ourselves with the fact that the document contains the words very, good, and bad but we don't really care that very comes before good, but not bad.

Bag of Word models are simple, require relatively little data, and work amazingly well considering the naivety of the model.

Note, the use of model here means representation. I'm not referring to a deep learning model or machine learning model in the specific sense. Rather, a model in this context means a way to represent text.

Given some document, that consists of a set of words, a strategy needs to be defined to convert a word to a number. We will look at a few strategies in a moment, but first we need to briefly discuss stemming, lemmatization, and stop words.

Stemming, lemmatization, and stopwords

Stemming and **lemmatization** are two different but very similar techniques that attempt to reduce every word to its base form, which simplifies the language model. For instance, if we were to stem the various forms of a cat, we'd make the transformation in this example:

cat, cats, cat's, cats' -> cat

The difference between lemmatization and stemming then becomes how we make this transformation. Stemming is done algorithmically. When applied to multiple forms of the same word, the extracted root should be the same most of the time. This concept can be contrasted with lemmatization, which uses a vocabulary with known bases and consideration for how the word was used.

Stemming is typically much faster than lemmatization. The Porter stemmer works very well in many cases, so you might consider that as a first safe choice for stemming.

Stop words are words that are very common in the language but carry very little semantic meaning. The canonical example is the word *the*. I just used it three times in my last sentence, but it really only held meaning once. Often we remove stop words to make the input a little more sparse.

Most BoW models benefit from stemming, lemmatization, and removing stop words. Sometimes word-embedding models, which we will talk about soon, also benefit from stemming or lemmatization. Word-embedding models will rarely benefit from the removal of stop words.

Count and TF-IDF vectorization

Count vectorization and **Term Frequency-Inverse Document Frequency** (**TTF-IDF**) are two different strategies to convert a bag of words into a feature vector suitable for input to a machine learning algorithm.

Count vectorization takes our set of words and creates a vector where each element represents one word in the corpus vocabulary. Naturally, the number of unique words in a set of documents might be quite large, and many documents may not contain any instances of a word present in the corpus. When this is the case, it's often very wise to use sparse matrices to represent these types of word vectors. When a word is present one or more times, the count vectorizer will simply count the number of times that word appears in the document and place that count in the position representing the word.

Using a count vectorizer, an entire corpus can be represented as a two-dimensional matrix, where each row is a document, each column is a word, and each element is then the count of that word in the document.

Let's walk through a quick example before moving on. Imagine a corpus with two documents like this:

```
docA = "the cat sat on my face"
docB = "the dog sat on my bed"
```

The corpus vocabulary is:

```
{'bed', 'cat', 'dog', 'face', 'my', 'on', 'sat', 'the'}
```

And so if we were to create a count embedding for this corpus, it would look like this:

	bed	cat	dog	face	my	on	sat	the
doc 0	0	1	0	1	1	1	1	1
doc 1	1	0	1	0	1	1	1	1

That's count vectorization. It's the simplest vectorization technique in our toolbox.

The problem with count vectorization is that we use many words that just don't have much meaning at all. In fact, the most commonly used word in the English language (*the*) makes up 7% of the words we speak, which is double the frequency of the next most popular word (*of*). The distribution of words in a language is a power law distribution, which is the basis for something called Zipf's law (https://en.wikipedia.org/wiki/Zipf%27s_law). If we construct our document matrix out of counts, we end up with numbers that don't contain much information, unless our goal was to see who uses *the* most often.

A better strategy is to weight the word based on its relative importance in the document. To do that we can use something called the TF-IDF.

The TF-IDF score of a word is:

$$score = tf(w) * idf(w)$$

In this formula:

$$tf(w) = Number\ of\ times\ the\ word\ w\ appears\ in\ a\ document/total\ words\ in\ the\ document$$

And n this formula:

$$idf(w) = log(Number\ of\ documents/number\ of\ documents\ that\ contain\ the\ word\ w)$$

If we were to compute the TF-IDF matrix for the same corpus, it would look like this:

	bed	cat	dog	face	my	on	sat	the
doc 0	0	0.116	0	0.116	0	0	0	0
doc 1	0.116	0	0.116	0	0	0	0	0

As you might notice, by weighting the words by their term frequency * inverse document frequency, we have canceled out the words that appear in all documents, which amplifies the words that are different. Document 0 is all about cats and faces, whereas document 1 is all about dogs and beds. This is exactly what we want for many classifiers.

Word embedding

Bag of Word models have a few less than ideal properties that are worth noting.

The first problem with the Bag of Word models we've previously looked at is that they don't consider the context of the word. They don't really consider the relationships that exist between the words in the document.

A second but related concern is that the assignment of words in the vector space is somewhat arbitrary. Information that might exist about the relation between two words in a corpus vocabulary might not be captured. For example, a model that has learned to process the word alligator can leverage very little of that learning when it comes across the word crocodile, even though both alligators and crocodiles are somewhat similar creatures that share many characteristics (bring on the herpetologist hate mail).

Lastly, because the vocabulary of a corpus can be very large and may not be present in all documents, BoW models tend to produce very sparse vectors.

Word-embedding models address these problems by learning a vector for each word where semantically similar words are mapped to (embedded in) nearby points. Additionally, we will represent the entire vocabulary in a much smaller vector space than we could with a BoW model. This provides dimensionality reduction and leaves us with a smaller and more dense vector that captures the word's semantic value.

Word-embedding models often provide quite a bit of lift over Bag of Word models in real-world document classification problems and semantic analysis problems because of this ability to preserve the semantic value of the word relative to other words in the corpus.

A quick example

If you're new to word embeddings, you might be feeling a little lost right now. Hang in there, it will become clearer in just a moment. Let's try a concrete example.

Using `word2vec`, a popular word-embedding model, we can start with the word cat and find it's 384 element vector, as shown in the following output code:

```
array([ 5.81600726e-01, 3.07168198e+00, 3.73339128e+00,
  2.83814788e-01, 2.79787600e-01, 2.29124355e+00,
  -2.14855480e+00, -1.22236431e+00, 2.20581269e+00,
  1.81546474e+00, 2.06929898e+00, -2.71712840e-01,...
```

I've cut the output short, but you get the idea. Every word in this model is converted into a 384-element vector. These vectors can be compared to evaluate the semantic similarity of words in a dataset.

Now that we have a vector for a cat, I'm going to compute the word vector for a dog and a lizard. I would suggest that cats are more like dogs than lizards. I should be able to measure the distance between the cat vector and dog vector, and then measure the distance between the cat vector and the lizard vector. While there are many ways to measure the distance between vectors, cosine similarity is probably the most commonly used for word vectors. In the following table, we're comparing the cosine similarity of cats versus dogs and lizards:

	Dog	Lizard
Cat	0.74	0.63

As expected, in our vector space, cats are closer to dogs in meaning than lizards.

Learning word embeddings with prediction

Word embeddings are calculated by using a neural network built specifically for the task. I'll cover an overview of that network here. Once the word embeddings for some corpora are calculated, they can be easily reused for other applications, so that makes this technique a candidate for transfer learning, similar to techniques we looked at in Chapter 8, *Transfer Learning with Pretrained CNNs*.

When we're done training this word-embedding network, the weights of the single hidden layer of our network will become a lookup table for our word embeddings. For each word in our vocabulary, we will have learned a vector for that word.

This hidden layer will contain fewer neurons than the input space, forcing the network to learn a compressed form of the information present in the input layer. This architecture very much resembles an auto-encoder; however, the technique is wrapped around a task that helps the network learn the semantic values of each word in a vector space.

The task we will use to train our embedding network with is predicting the probability of some target word appearing within a window of distance from the training word. For example, if *koala* was our input word and *marsupial* was our target word, we'd want to know the probability of these two words being near each other.

The input layer for this task will be one hot encoded vector of every word in the vocabulary. The output layer will be a `softmax` layer of the same size, as shown in the following figure:

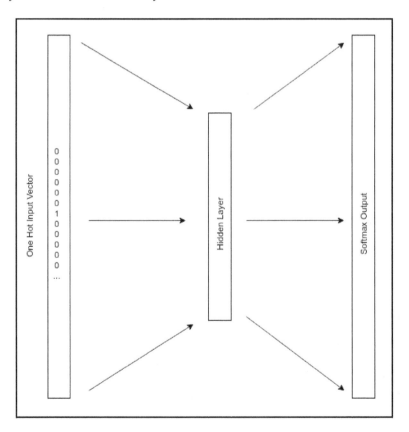

This network results in a hidden layer with a weight matrix of shape [**vocabulary x neurons**]. For example, if we had 20,000 unique words in our corpus and 300 neurons in our hidden layer, our hidden layer weight matrix would be 20,000 x 300. Once we save these weights to disk, we have a 300 element vector that we can use to represent each word. These vectors can then be used to represent words when training other models.

There is most certainly more to training word-embedding networks than this and I'm intentionally oversimplifying the quick reference style.

 If you'd like to learn more, I recommend starting by reading *Distributed Representations of Words and Phrases and their Compositionality* by Mikolov et al. (`https://papers.nips.cc/paper/5021-distributed-representations-of-words-and-phrases-and-their-compositionality.pdf`). This paper describes a popular way to create word embeddings called `word2vec`.

Learning word embeddings with counting

Another way to learn word embeddings is by counting. The **Global Vectors for Word Representation** or **GloVe** is an algorithm created by Pennington et al. (`https://nlp.stanford.edu/projects/glove/`).

GloVe works by creating a very large matrix of word co-occurrences. For some corpora, this is essentially a count of the number of times two words occur nearby each other. The algorithm authors weight this count by how close the words are so that words that are close together contribute more to each count. Once this co-occurrence matrix is created, it's decomposed into a smaller space, resulting in a matrix that is words x features big.

Interestingly enough, the results from `word2vec` and GloVe are very similar and can be used interchangeably. GloVe vectors, prebuilt from a dataset of 6 billion words, are distributed by Stanford and are a commonly used source of word vectors. We will be using GloVe vectors later in this chapter.

Getting from words to documents

If you've been reading carefully, you might have noticed a gap that I haven't closed. Word-embedding models create a vector for each word. Comparatively, BoW models create a vector for each document. So then, how can we use word-embedding models for document classification?

One naive way might be to take the vectors for all the words in our document and compute the mean. We might interpret this value to be the mean semantic value for the document. In practice, this solution is often used and it can yield good results. However, it is not always superior to BoW embedding models. Consider the phrases *dog bites man* and *man bites dog*. Hopefully, you'll agree with me that those are two very different statements; however, if we averaged their word vectors, they would have the same value. This leads us to a few other strategies we might employ to engineer features from a document, such as using the mean, max, and min of each vector.

A better idea for getting from words to documents was presented in *Distributed Representations of Sentences and Documents* by Le and Mikolov (`https://arxiv.org/abs/1405.4053`). Building on their ideas from `word2vec`, in this paper a paragraph identifier is added to the input of the neural network we described for learning word vectors. Using the words in a piece of text along with the document ID allows the network to learn to embed variable length documents in a vector space. This technique is called **doc2vec** and can work well as a technique for topic modeling as well as creating input features for a model.

Lastly, many deep learning frameworks incorporate the concept of an embedding layer. Embedding layers allow you to learn an embedding space as part of the overall task the network is performing. An embedding layer is probably the best choice for vectorizing text when using a deep neural network. Let's take a look at embedding layers next.

Keras embedding layer

The **Keras embedding layer** allows us to learn a vector space representation of an input word, like we did in `word2vec`, as we train our model. Using the functional API, the Keras embedding layer is always the second layer in the network, coming after the input layer.

The embedding layer needs the following three arguments:

- `input_dim`: The size of the vocabulary of the corpus.
- `output_dim`: The size of the vector space we want to learn. This would correspond to the number of neurons in `word2vec` hidden layer.
- `input_length`: The number of words in the text we're going to use in each observation. In the examples that follow, we will use a fixed size based on the longest text we need to send and we will pad smaller documents with 0s.

An embedding layer will output a 2D matrix for each input document that contains one vector for each word in the sequence specified by `input_length`.

As an example, we may have an embedding layer that looks like this:

```
Embedding(input_dim=10000, output_dim=128, input_length=10)
```

In this case, the output of this layer would be a 2D matrix of shape 10 x 128, where each document's 10 words would have a 128-element vector associated with it.

Sequences of words like this serve as excellent inputs to LSTMs. An LSTM layer can immediately follow an embedding layer. We can treat these 10 rows from the embedding layer as sequenced input for an LSTM, exactly like we did in the previous chapter. I'll be using an LSTM in the first example for this chapter, so if you arrived here without reading Chapter 9, *Training an RNN from scratch*, you might want to take a moment to refresh yourself on the operation of LSTMs, which can be found there.

If we wanted to connect an embedding layer directly to a dense layer, we would need to flatten it, but you probably don't want to do that. Using an LSTM is usually a better choice if you have a sequenced text though. There is one other interesting option we should explore though.

1D CNNs for natural language processing

Way back in Chapter 7, *Training a CNN From Scratch*, we used convolutions to slide a window over regions of an image to learn complex visual features. This allowed us to learn important local visual features, regardless of where in the picture those features might have been, and then hierarchically learn more and more complex features as our network got deeper. We typically used a *3 x 3* or *5 x 5* filter on a 2D or 3D image. You may want to review Chapter 7, *Training a CNN From Scratch*, if you are feeling rusty on your understanding of convolution layers and how they work.

It turns out that we can use the same strategy on a sequence of words. Here, our 2D matrix is the output from an embedding layer. Each row represents a word, and all the elements in that row are its word vector. Continuing with the preceding example, we would have a 10 x 128 vector, where there are 10 words in a row, and each word is represented by a 128 element vector space. We most certainly can slide a filter over these words.

The convolutional filter size changes for NLP problems. When we're building networks to solve NLP problems, our filter will be as wide as the word vector. The height of the filter can vary, with typical ranges being between 2 and 5. A height of 5 would mean that we're sliding our filter across five words at a time.

It turns out that for many NLP problems, CNNs work very well and they're much faster than LSTMs. It's hard to give exact rules about when to use an RNN/LSTM and when to use a CNN. Generally, if your problem requires a state, or learning something from very far back in the sequence, you're likely to be better off with an LSTM. If your problem requires detecting a particular set of words that describe the text, or a semantic feeling for a document, then a CNN will likely solve your problem faster and possibly better.

Case studies for document classifications

Since I have presented two viable alternatives for document classifications, this chapter will contain two separate examples for document classification. Both will use embedding layers. One will use an LSTM and the other will use a CNN.

We will also compare the performance between learning an embedding layer and, starting with someone else's weights, applying a transfer learning approach.

The code for both of these examples can be found in the Chapter10 folder in the book's Git repo. Some of the data and the GloVe vectors will need to be downloaded separately. Instructions to do so exist in comments within the code.

Sentiment analysis with Keras embedding layers and LSTMs

The first case study in this chapter will demonstrate sentiment analysis. In this example, we will get to apply most of the things we have learned in the chapter.

We will be using a dataset built into Keras from the **Internet Movie DataBase** (**IMDB**). This dataset contains 25,000 movies reviews, each labeled by sentiment. Positive reviews are labeled 1 and negative reviews are labeled 0. Every word in this dataset has been replaced with an integer that identifies it. Each review has been encoded as a sequence of word indexes.

Our goal will be to classify movie reviews as either a positive or negative review using only the text in that review.

Preparing the data

Because we're using a built-in dataset, Keras takes care of a great deal of the mundane work we'd need to do around tokenizing, stemming, stop words, and converting our word tokens into numeric tokens. `keras.datasets.imbd` will give us a list of lists, each list containing a variable length sequence of integers representing the words in the review. We will define our data using the following code:

```
def load_data(vocab_size):
    data = dict()
    data["vocab_size"] = vocab_size
    (data["X_train"], data["y_train"]), (data["X_test"], data["y_test"]) =
    imdb.load_data(num_words=vocab_size)
    return data
```

We can load our data by calling `load_data` and choosing a maximum size for our vocabulary. For this example, I'll use 20,000 words as the vocabulary size.

If you needed to do this step by hand, to make the example code work with your own problem, you can use the `keras.preprocessing.text.Tokenizer` class, which we will also cover in the next example. We will load our data using the following code:

```
data = load_data(20000)
```

As a next step, I'd like each of these sequences to be the same length, and I need this list of lists to be a 2D matrix, where each review is a row and each column is a word in the review. To get each list to be the same size, I will pad the shorter sequences with 0s. The LSTM we will use later will learn to ignore those 0s, which is of course very convenient for us.

This padding operation is fairly common, enough so that it is built into Keras. We can use `keras.preprocessing.sequence.pad_sequences` to accomplish this, using the following code:

```
def pad_sequences(data):
    data["X_train"] = sequence.pad_sequences(data["X_train"])
    data["sequence_length"] = data["X_train"].shape[1]
    data["X_test"] = sequence.pad_sequences(data["X_test"],
maxlen=data["sequence_length"])
    return data
```

Invoking this function will convert our lists of lists to equal length sequences and conveniently convert our list of lists into a 2D matrix, as follows:

```
data = pad_sequences(data)
```

Input and embedding layer architecture

In the last chapter, we trained an LSTM with a set of lags from a time series. Here our lags are really the words in a sequence. We will use these words to predict the sentiment of the reviewer. In order to get from a sequence of words to an input vector that considers the semantic value of those words, we can use an embedding layer.

Using the Keras functional API, the embedding layer is always the second layer in the network after the input layer. Let's look at how these two layers fit together:

```
input = Input(shape=(sequence_length,), name="Input")
embedding = Embedding(input_dim=vocab_size, output_dim=embedding_dim,
                      input_length=sequence_length,
name="embedding")(input)
```

Our input layer needs to know the sequence length, which corresponds to the number of columns in the input matrix.

The embedding layer will use the input layer; however, it needs to know the overall corpus vocabulary size, the size of the vector space we're embedding those words into, and the sequence length.

We've defined a vocabulary of 20,000 words, the data has a sequence length of 2,494, and we've specified an embedding dimension of 100.

Putting this all together, the embedding layer will go from a 20,000 input one hot vector to a 2,494 x 100 2D matrix for each document yielding the vector space embedding for each word in the sequence. As the model learns, the embedding layer will learn along the way. Pretty cool, right?

LSTM layer

I'm only going to use one LSTM layer here, with just 10 neurons, as shown in the following code:

```
lstm1 = LSTM(10, activation='tanh', return_sequences=False,
             dropout=0.2, recurrent_dropout=0.2, name='lstm1')(embedding)
```

Why am I using such a small LSTM layer? As as you're about to see, this model is going to struggle with overfitting. Even just 10 LSTM units are able to learn the training data a little too well. The answer to this problem is likely to add data, but we really can't, so keeping the network structure simple is a good idea.

That leads us to the use of dropout. I will use both dropout and recurrent dropout on this layer. We haven't talked about recurrent dropout yet so let's cover that now. Normal dropout, applied on an LSTM layer in this way, will randomly mask inputs to the LSTM. Recurrent dropout randomly turns on and off memory between the *unrolled* cells in an LSTM unit/neuron. As always, dropout is a hyperparameter and you'll need to search for an optimal value.

Because our inputs are document based, and because there isn't any context, we need to remember between documents that this is a great time to use a stateless LSTM.

Output layer

In this example we're predicting a binary target. As before, we can use a dense layer with a single sigmoid neuron to accomplish this binary classification task:

```
output = Dense(1, activation='sigmoid', name='sigmoid')(lstm1)
```

Putting it all together

Now let's look at the entire network, now that we understand the parts. The network is shown in the following code for your reference:

```
def build_network(vocab_size, embedding_dim, sequence_length):
    input = Input(shape=(sequence_length,), name="Input")
    embedding = Embedding(input_dim=vocab_size,
        output_dim=embedding_dim, input_length=sequence_length,
            name="embedding")(input)
    lstm1 = LSTM(10, activation='tanh', return_sequences=False,
        dropout=0.2, recurrent_dropout=0.2, name='lstm1')(embedding)
    output = Dense(1, activation='sigmoid', name='sigmoid')(lstm1)
    model = Model(inputs=input, outputs=output)
    model.compile(optimizer='adam', loss='binary_crossentropy',
metrics=['accuracy'])
    return model
```

As we have with other binary classification tasks, we can use binary cross-entropy. Note that because we're connecting our LSTM layer to a dense layer, we need to set `return_sequences` to `False`, as we discussed in `Chapter 9`, *Training an RNN from Scratch*.

To make this bit of code reusable, we make the vocabulary size, embedding dimension, and sequence length configurable. If you were going to search for hyperparameters, you may also wish to parameterize `dropout`, `recurrent_dropout`, and the number of LSTM neurons.

Training the network

Now that my sentiment analysis network is built, it's time to train:

```
data = load_data(20000)
data = pad_sequences(data)
model = build_network(vocab_size=data["vocab_size"],
                      embedding_dim=100,
                      sequence_length=data["sequence_length"])

callbacks = create_callbacks("sentiment")

model.fit(x=data["X_train"], y=data["y_train"],
          batch_size=32,
          epochs=10,
          validation_data=(data["X_test"], data["y_test"]),
          callbacks=callbacks)
```

Keeping all of my training parameters and data in a single dictionary like this is just really a question of style and less about function. You may prefer to handle everything separately. I like using a dictionary for everything because it keeps me from passing big lists of parameters back and forth.

Since we're using a stateless LSTM, we're resetting cell memory in every batch. My belief is that we can probably reset cell states between documents without penalty, so then the batch size really becomes about performance. I'm using 32 observation batches here, but 128 observation batches yield similar results with a slight performance boost as long as your GPU memory allows it.

Performance

Let's take a look at how our network is doing, from the following screenshot. When you inspect these graphs, keep a close eye on the scale on the *y*-axis. While the swings look dramatic, they aren't that big:

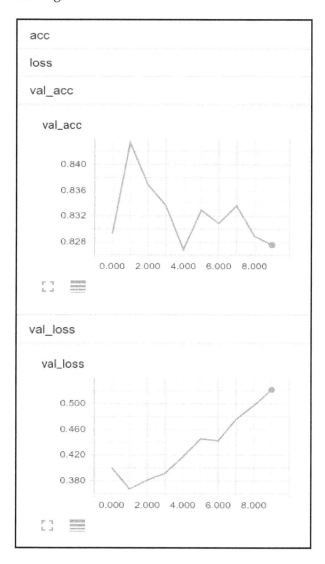

The first thing to notice here is that at epoch 1 the network is doing a pretty good job. After that, it rapidly begins to overfit. Overall though, I think our results are pretty good. At epoch 1, we're correctly predicting the sentiment about 86% of the time on the validation set.

While this case study covers many of the topics that we've discussed so far in the chapter, let's look at one more where we can compare using pre-trained word vectors for our embedding layer with word vectors we learn ourselves.

Document classification with and without GloVe

In this example, we're going to use a somewhat famous text classification problem known as the **20 newsgroup problem** (http://www.cs.cmu.edu/afs/cs.cmu.edu/project/theo-20/www/data/news20.html). In this problem, we are given 19,997 documents, each belonging to a newsgroup. Our goal is to use the text of the post to predict which newsgroup the text belongs in. For the millennials among us, a newsgroup is sort of the precursor to **Reddit** (but it's probably closer to the great-great-great grandfather of Reddit). The topics covered in those newsgroups vary greatly and include such topics as politics, religion, and operating systems, all of which you should avoid discussing in polite company. These posts are fairly long and there are 174,074 unique words in the corpus.

This time I'm going to build two versions of the model. In the first version, we will use an embedding layer and we will learn the embedding space, just like we did in the previous example. In the second version, I will use GloVe vectors as the weights for the embedding layer. I'll then spend some time at the end comparing and contrasting the two methods.

Lastly, instead of an LSTM, in this example, we will use a 1D CNN.

Preparing the data

When working with text documents like this it can take a lot of mundane code to get you where you want to be. I'm including this example as a way to handle the problem. Once you understand what's going on here, you will be able to reuse much of it in future problems and shorten your development time, so it's worth the consideration.

The following function is going to take the top-level directory where the 20 newsgroup texts live. Within that directory, there will be 20 individual directories, each with files. Each file is a newsgroup post:

```
def load_data(text_data_dir, vocab_size, sequence_length,
validation_split=0.2):
```

```
data = dict()
data["vocab_size"] = vocab_size
data["sequence_length"] = sequence_length

# second, prepare text samples and their labels
print('Processing text dataset')

texts = []   # list of text samples
labels_index = {}   # dictionary mapping label name to numeric id
labels = []   # list of label ids
for name in sorted(os.listdir(text_data_dir)):
    path = os.path.join(text_data_dir, name)
    if os.path.isdir(path):
        label_id = len(labels_index)
        labels_index[name] = label_id
        for fname in sorted(os.listdir(path)):
            if fname.isdigit():
                fpath = os.path.join(path, fname)
                if sys.version_info < (3,):
                    f = open(fpath)
                else:
                    f = open(fpath, encoding='latin-1')
                t = f.read()
                i = t.find('\n\n')   # skip header
                if 0 < i:
                    t = t[i:]
                texts.append(t)
                f.close()
                labels.append(label_id)
print('Found %s texts.' % len(texts))
data["texts"] = texts
data["labels"] = labels
return data
```

For each directory, we will take the directory name and add it to a dictionary mapping it to a number. This number is going to become the value we care to predict, our label. We will keep that list of labels in data["labels"].

Likewise, for the texts, we will open each file, parse out just the relevant text, ignoring the junk about who posted in the information. We will then store the text in data["texts"]. It's very important to remove the part of the header that identifies the newsgroup, by the way; that's cheating!

In the end, we are left with a list of texts and a corresponding list of labels; however, at this point, each of those texts is a string. The next thing we need to do is split these strings into word tokens, convert those tokens into numeric tokens, and pad the sequences so that they're the same length. This is pretty much what we did in the previous example; however, in our previous example, the data came pre-tokenized. I'll use this function to accomplish the task, as shown in the following code:

```
def tokenize_text(data):
    tokenizer = Tokenizer(num_words=data["vocab_size"])
    tokenizer.fit_on_texts(data["texts"])
    data["tokenizer"] = tokenizer
    sequences = tokenizer.texts_to_sequences(data["texts"])

    word_index = tokenizer.word_index
    print('Found %s unique tokens.' % len(word_index))

    data["X"] = pad_sequences(sequences, maxlen=data["sequence_length"])
    data["y"] = to_categorical(np.asarray(data["labels"]))
    print('Shape of data tensor:', data["X"].shape)
    print('Shape of label tensor:', data["y"].shape)

    # texts and labels aren't needed anymore
    data.pop("texts", None)
    data.pop("labels", None)
    return data
```

Here we're taking that list of texts and tokenizing them with `keras.preprocessing.text.Tokenizer`. After that, we're padding them to be equal length. Finally, we're converting the numeric labels to `one_hot` format, as we have in other multiclass classification problems with Keras.

We're almost done with the data; however, lastly, we need to take our text and labels and randomly split that data into a train, validation, and test set, as shown in the following code. I don't have much data to work with so I'm going to make the choice here to be fairly stingy on `test` and `val`. If my sample is too small, I might not get a good understanding of actual model performance, so be careful when you're doing this:

```
def train_val_test_split(data):

    data["X_train"], X_test_val, data["y_train"], y_test_val =
train_test_split(data["X"],
data["y"],
test_size=0.2,
random_state=42)
    data["X_val"], data["X_test"], data["y_val"], data["y_test"] =
train_test_split(X_test_val,
```

```
    y_test_val,
    test_size=0.25,
    random_state=42)
        return data
```

Loading pretrained word vectors

As I have just mentioned, I'm going to use a Keras embedding layer. For the second version of the model, we will initialize the weights of the embedding layer with the GloVe word vectors we covered previously in the chapter. To do so, we will need to load those weights from disk and put them into a suitable 2D matrix that the layer can use as weights. We will cover that operation here.

When you download the GloVe vectors, you'll see that you have several text files in the directory you unzipped the download in. Each of these files corresponds to a separate set of dimensions; however, in all cases, these vectors were developed using the same common corpus containing 6 billion unique words (hence the title GloVe.6B). I will demonstrate using glove.6B.100d.txt file. Inside glove.6B.100d.txt every line is a single word vector. On that line, you will find the word and a 100 dimension vector associated to it. The word and the elements of the vector are stored as text and separated by spaces.

To get this data into a usable state, we will start by loading it from disk. We will then split the line into its first component, the word, and the elements of the vector. Once we're done with that, we will convert the vector into an array. Lastly, we will store the array as a value in a dictionary, using the word as the key for that value. The following code illustrates this process:

```
def load_word_vectors(glove_dir):
    print('Indexing word vectors.')

    embeddings_index = {}
    f = open(os.path.join(glove_dir, 'glove.6B.100d.txt'),
            encoding='utf8')
    for line in f:
        values = line.split()
        word = values[0]
        coefs = np.asarray(values[1:], dtype='float32')
        embeddings_index[word] = coefs
    f.close()

    print('Found %s word vectors.' % len(embeddings_index))
    return embeddings_index
```

Once we run this, we will have a dictionary called `embeddings_index` that contains the GloVe words as keys and their vectors as values. The Keras embedding layer needs a 2D matrix as input, however, not a dictionary, so we will need to manipulate our dictionary into a matrix, using the following code:

```
def embedding_index_to_matrix(embeddings_index, vocab_size, embedding_dim,
word_index):
    print('Preparing embedding matrix.')

    # prepare embedding matrix
    num_words = min(vocab_size, len(word_index))
    embedding_matrix = np.zeros((num_words, embedding_dim))
    for word, i in word_index.items():
        if i >= vocab_size:
            continue
        embedding_vector = embeddings_index.get(word)
        if embedding_vector is not None:
            # words not found in embedding index will be all-zeros.
            embedding_matrix[i] = embedding_vector
    return embedding_matrix
```

I know all this munging might seem terrible, and it is, but the authors of GloVe are quite well-intentioned in how they distribute these word vectors. They hope to make these vectors consumable by anyone using any programming language and to that end the text format will be quite appreciated. Besides, if you're a practicing data scientist, you will be used to this!

Now that we have our vectors present as a 2D matrix, we're ready to use them in a Keras embedding layer. Our prep work is done, so now let's build the network.

Input and embedding layer architecture

We're going to format the API just a little differently here than we did in the previous example. This slightly different structure will make the using of pretrained vectors in the embedding layer a little bit easier. We will discuss these structural changes in the following sections.

Without GloVe vectors

Let's demonstrate the code for an `embedding` layer without pretrained word vectors first. This code should look almost the same as the code in the previous example:

```
sequence_input = Input(shape=(sequence_length,), dtype='int32')
embedding_layer = Embedding(input_dim=vocab_size,
```

```
                            output_dim=embedding_dim,
                            input_length=sequence_length,
                            name="embedding")(sequence_input)
```

With GloVe vectors

Now let's compare that to the code that includes pretrained GloVe vectors encoded in a 2D matrix:

```
sequence_input = Input(shape=(sequence_length,), dtype='int32')
embedding_layer = Embedding(input_dim=vocab_size,
                            output_dim=embedding_dim,
                            weights=[embedding_matrix],
                            input_length=sequence_length,
                            trainable=False,
                            name="embedding")(sequence_input)
```

For the most part, this code looks equivalent. There are two key differences:

- We initialize the layer weights to be contained in the GloVe matrix that we assembled with `weights=[embedding_matrix]`.
- We also set the layer to `trainable=False`. This will prevent us from updating our weights. You may wish to fine tune the weights in a similar way to how we fine tuned the CNN we built in `Chapter 8`, *Transfer Learning with Pretrained CNNs*, but most of the time that isn't necessary or helpful.

Convolution layers

For one-dimensional convolutional, layers we can use `keras.layers.Conv1D`. We will need to use `MaxPooling1D` layers to go along with our `Conv1D` layers, as shown in the following code:

```
x = Conv1D(128, 5, activation='relu')(embedding_layer)
x = MaxPooling1D(5)(x)
x = Conv1D(128, 5, activation='relu')(x)
x = MaxPooling1D(5)(x)
x = Conv1D(128, 5, activation='relu')(x)
x = GlobalMaxPooling1D()(x)
```

For the `Conv1D` layers, the first integer argument is the number of units and the second is the filter size. Our filter only has one dimension, hence the name 1D convolution. Our window size in the preceding example is 5.

The `MaxPooling1D` layers that I'm using will also use a window size of 5. The same rules apply for the pooling layers in a 1D implementation.

After the last convolutional layer, we apply the `GlobalMaxPooling1D` layer. This layer is a special implementation of max pooling that will take the output of the last `Conv1D` layer, a [batch x 35 x 128] tensor, and pool it across time steps to [batch x 128]. This is commonly done in NLP networks and is similar in intent to the use of the `Flatten()` layer in image-based convolutional networks. This layer serves as the bridge between the convolutional layers and the dense layers.

Output layer

The output layer in this example looks like any other multiclass classification. I've included a single dense layer before the output layer as well, as shown in the following code:

```
x = Dense(128, activation='relu')(x)
preds = Dense(20, activation='softmax')(x)
```

Putting it all together

As before, we will show the entire neural network structure here. Note that this structure is for the version of the model that includes GloVe vectors:

```
def build_model(vocab_size, embedding_dim, sequence_length,
embedding_matrix):

    sequence_input = Input(shape=(sequence_length,), dtype='int32')
    embedding_layer = Embedding(input_dim=vocab_size,
                                output_dim=embedding_dim,
                                weights=[embedding_matrix],
                                input_length=sequence_length,
                                trainable=False,
                                name="embedding")(sequence_input)
    x = Conv1D(128, 5, activation='relu')(embedding_layer)
    x = MaxPooling1D(5)(x)
    x = Conv1D(128, 5, activation='relu')(x)
    x = MaxPooling1D(5)(x)
    x = Conv1D(128, 5, activation='relu')(x)
    x = GlobalMaxPooling1D()(x)
    x = Dense(128, activation='relu')(x)
    preds = Dense(20, activation='softmax')(x)
    model = Model(sequence_input, preds)
    model.compile(loss='categorical_crossentropy',
```

```
                  optimizer='adam',
                  metrics=['accuracy'])
    return model
```

I'm using `adam`, `categorical_crossentropy`, and `accuracy` here again. While there are many new topics presented in this chapter, hopefully it's somewhat comforting to see what remains constant.

Training

With all the code put together, training can be done in just a few lines, as shown in the following code:

```
glove_dir = os.path.join(BASE_DIR, 'glove.6B')
text_data_dir = os.path.join(BASE_DIR, '20_newsgroup')
embeddings_index = load_word_vectors(glove_dir)

data = load_data(text_data_dir, vocab_size=20000, sequence_length=1000)
data = tokenize_text(data)
data = train_val_test_split(data)
data["embedding_dim"] = 100
data["embedding_matrix"] =
embedding_index_to_matrix(embeddings_index=embeddings_index,
vocab_size=data["vocab_size"],
embedding_dim=data["embedding_dim"],
word_index=data["tokenizer"].word_index)

callbacks = create_callbacks("newsgroups-pretrained")
model = build_model(vocab_size=data["vocab_size"],
                    embedding_dim=data['embedding_dim'],
                    sequence_length=data['sequence_length'],
                    embedding_matrix=data['embedding_matrix'])

model.fit(data["X_train"], data["y_train"],
          batch_size=128,
          epochs=10,
          validation_data=(data["X_val"], data["y_val"]),
          callbacks=callbacks)
```

Note that we're only training for 10 epochs, it doesn't really take long for us to minimize loss for this problem.

Performance

And here we are at the moment of truth. Let's see how I did. More importantly, let's compare GloVe vectors to learned vectors for this problem.

The orange line in the following screenshot corresponds to the learned embedded layer and the blue line corresponds to the GloVe vectors:

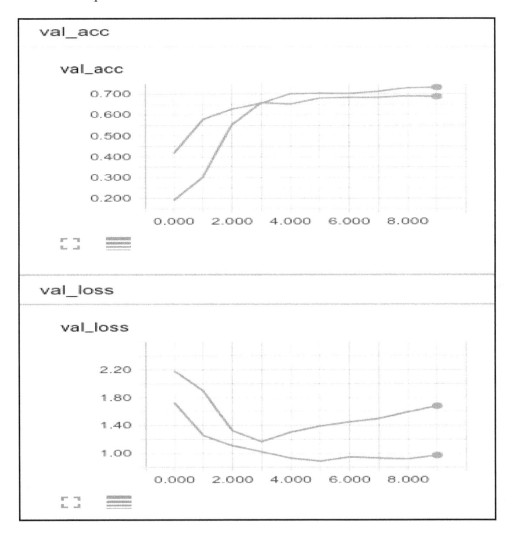

Not only does the GloVe pretrained network learn faster, but it also performs better, throughout every epoch. Overall these networks seem to do a good job learning the document classification task. They're both beginning to overfit after about the fifth epoch; however, the GloVe model is more robust against overfitting than the network trained without GloVe.

> As a general rule, I would recommend using transfer learning whenever and wherever possible. That's true for images and for text.

If you're working though these examples with me, I would recommend that you attempt the same problem with an LSTM. I think you'll find the problem more difficult to solve, and harder to manage overfitting, when using an LSTM.

Summary

In this chapter, we looked at document classification in its general form, and in the specific case of sentiment analysis. In doing so, we covered a great many NLP topics, including Bag of Word models, Vector Space models, and the relative merits of each. We also looked at using LSTMs and 1D convolutions for text analysis. We ended by training two separate document classifiers, applying everything we talked about with practical examples.

In the next chapter, we will talk about a very cool natural language model that will allow us to actually generate words, called a **sequence-to-sequence model**.

11
Training Seq2Seq Models

In the last chapter, we talked about document classification, and a special case of document classification called **sentiment classification**. In doing so, we got to talk quite a bit about vectorization.

In this chapter, we're going to keep talking about solving NLP problems, but instead of classifying, we're going to generate new sequences of words.

We will cover the following topics in this chapter:

- Sequence-to-sequence models
- Machine translation

Sequence-to-sequence models

The networks that we've looked at so far have done some truly amazing things. But they've all had one pretty big limitation: they can only be applied to problems where the output is of a fixed and well-known size.

Sequence-to-sequence models are able to map sequences of inputs to sequences of outputs with variable lengths.

You might also see the terms sequence-to-sequence or even **Seq2Seq**. These are all terms for sequence-to-sequence models.

When using a sequence-to-sequence model, we will take a sequence in and get a sequence out in exchange. These sequences don't have to be the same length. Sequence-to-sequence models allow us to learn a mapping between the input sequence and the output sequence.

There are a variety of applications where sequence-to-sequence models might be useful, and we will talk about those applications next.

Sequence-to-sequence model applications

Sequence-to-sequence models have quite a few practical applications.

Perhaps the most practical application is **machine translation**. We can use machine translation to take a phrase in one language as input and output that phrase in another language. Machine translation is an important service that we depend on more and more. Thanks to advances in computer vision and machine translation, we can listen to a language we don't know, or look at a sign in a language we don't know, and have a pretty good translation almost immediately on our smartphone. Sequence-to-sequence networks really have gotten us very close to Douglas Adam's imagined babel fish from *The Hitchhiker's Guide to the Galaxy*.

Question-answering can also be accomplished in whole or in part by sequence-to-sequence models, where we can imagine the question as an input sequence and the answer as an output sequence. The most generalized application of question-answering is chat. If you support an enterprise with a call center, you have thousands or maybe millions of question/answer pairs that pass over the phone every day. That's the perfect training set for a sequence-to-sequence chat bot.

There are several nuanced forms of this question-answering idea that we can exploit. Every day, I get roughly 3.4 billion emails. Of those, I probably only need to read 20-30 (and that's a classification task); however, my responses to those emails are rarely novel. I could almost certainly create a sequence-to-sequence network that would write my emails for me, or at least draft a response. I think that we are beginning to see behavior like this built in to our favorite email programs already, and more fully automatic responses are sure to come.

Another great use of sequence-to-sequence networks is in automatic text summarization. Imagine a set of research papers or a big stack of journal articles. All those papers probably have an abstract. This is just another translation problem. We can use a sequence-to-sequence network to generate an abstract, given some paper. The network can learn to summarize documents in this manner.

Later in the chapter, we will implement a sequence-to-sequence network to do machine translation. Before we do that though, let's understand how this network architecture works.

Sequence-to-sequence model architecture

The key to understanding sequence-to-sequence model architecture is understanding that the architecture is built to allow the input sequence to vary in length from the output sequence. The entire input sequence can then be used to predict an output sequence of varying length.

To do that, the network is divided into two separate parts, each part consists of one or more LSTM layers responsible for half of the task. We discussed LSTMs back in `Chapter 9`, *Training an RNN from scratch*, if you'd like a refresher on their operation. We will learn about each of these two parts in the following sections.

Encoders and decoders

Sequence-to-sequence models are composed of two separate components, an encoder and a decoder:

- **Encoder**: The encoder portion of the model takes an input sequence and returns an output and the network's internal state. We don't really care about the output; we only want to keep the encoder's state, which is the memory of the input sequence.
- **Decoder**: The decoder portion of the model then takes the state from the encoder, which is called the **context** or **conditioning**, as input. It then predicts the target sequence at each time step given the output of the previous time step.

The encoder and decoder then work together as pictured below, taking an input sequence and generating an output sequence. As you can see, we use special characters to represent the start and end of the sequence.

We know to stop generating output once the end of sequence character, which I'll call **<EOS>** is generated:

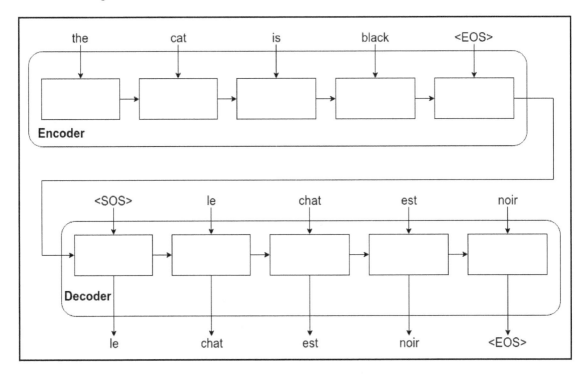

While this example covers machine translation, other applications of sequence-to-sequence learning work exactly the same way.

Characters versus words

Sequence-to-sequence models can be built at either the character level or the word level. A word-level sequence-to-sequence model will take words as the atomic unit of the input, and a character-level model will take characters as the atomic unit of the input.

So, which should you use? Typically, the best results are obtained from word-level models. That said, predicting the most probable next word in a sequence requires a `softmax` layer as wide as the vocabulary of the problem. This results in a very wide, highly dimensional problem.

Character-level models are much smaller. There are 26 letters in the alphabet but there are about 171,000 English words in common use.

For the problem we present in this chapter, I'll use a character-level model because I value your AWS budget. Converting to words is fairly straightforward, with the majority of the complexity being in the data prep, which is an exercise left to the reader.

Teacher forcing

As seen in the illustration above, when predicting an output at some place in the sequence $y_{t(n)}$, we use $y_{t(n-1)}$ as the input to the LSTM. We then use the output from this time step to predict $y_{t(n+1)}$.

The problem with doing this in training is that if $y_{t(n-1)}$ is wrong, $y_{t(n)}$ will be even more wrong. This chain of increasing wrongness can make things very very slow to train.

A somewhat obvious solution to this problem is to replace each sequence prediction at each time step with the actual correct sequence at that time step. So, rather than using the LSTM prediction for $y_{t(n-1)}$, we would use the actual value from the training set.

We can give the model's training process a boost by using this concept, which happens to be called **teacher forcing**.

Teacher forcing can sometimes make it difficult for our model to robustly generate sequences outside of those seen in training, but in general the technique can be helpful.

Attention

Attention is another helpful training trick that can be implemented in sequence-to-sequence models. Attention lets the decoder see the hidden state at each step of the input sequence. This lets the network focus on (or pay attention to) specific inputs, which speeds training and can provide some lift in model accuracy. Attention is typically a good thing; however, at the time of writing, Keras doesn't have attention built in. Keras does currently have a pull request pending for a custom attention layer though. I suspect that, very soon, support for attention will be built in to Keras.

Translation metrics

Knowing whether a translation is good or not is somewhat difficult. A common metric for the quality of a machine translation is called **Bilingual Evaluation Understudy** (**BLEU**), and it was created originally by Papineni and others in BLEU: a Method for Automatic Evaluation of Machine Translation (`http://aclweb.org/anthology/P/P02/P02-1040.pdf`). BLEU is a modified application of classification precision that's ngram based. If you'd like to use BLEU to measure the quality of your translations, the TensorFlow team has published a script that can compute a BLEU score given a corpus of ground truth translations and machine-predicted translations. You can find that script at `https://github.com/tensorflow/nmt/blob/master/nmt/scripts/bleu.py`.

Machine translation

Je ne parle pas français. That's how you say I don't speak French in English. Just about two years ago, I found myself in Paris, speaking almost no French. I had read a book and listened to some DVDs before I went, but even after a few months of practice, my mastery of the French language was pretty much pathetic. Then, on the very first morning of my trip, I woke up and walked into a nearby *boulangerie* (a French or French-style bakery) for my breakfast and morning coffee. I did my best at *Bonjour, parlez-vous anglais?* They didn't speak a bit of English, or perhaps they were enjoying my struggle. Either way, when my breakfast depended on my mastery of French, I was more motivated to struggle through *Je voudrais un pain au chocolat* (translation: *I would like one of those delicious chocolate bread things*) than I had ever been. I was quickly learning to map between English sequences and French sequences, driven by the ultimate cost function—my stomach.

In this case study, we're going to teach a computer to speak French. In a few hours of training, this model will be able to speak French better than me. That's pretty amazing when you think about it. I'm going to train a computer to take on a task that I myself can't do. Of course, maybe you do speak French and this doesn't impress you very much, in which case I'll quote the famous American actor Adam Sandler as Billy Madison: Well, it was tough for me, so back off!

Much of this example comes from, and is inspired by, a blog post by Francois Chollet titled A ten-minute introduction to sequence-to-sequence learning (`https://blog.keras.io/a-ten-minute-introduction-to-sequence-to-sequence-learning-in-keras.html`). While I doubt I can improve upon this work, my hope in using this example is to take a slightly longer than 10 minute look at sequence-to-sequence networks so that you have all the understanding you require to implement your own.

As always, the code for this chapter can be found in the book's Git repo, under `Chapter11`. The data that you'll need for this example is found at `http://www.manythings.org/anki/`, which archives many datasets of bilingual sentence pairs, which we will talk about in detail shortly. The file I'm going to be using is `fra-eng.zip`. It's a collection of English/French sentence pairs. You can easily pick another language if you want, without much modification.

In this case study, we will build a network that can learn a French sentence given some English sentence. This will be a character-level sequence-to-sequence model with teacher forcing.

What I hope to end up with is something that looks a great deal like a translation service you might find on the web or download to your phone.

Understanding the data

The data that we're working with is a text file. Each line has a single English phrase and its French translation, separated by a single tab, as shown in the following code:

```
Ignore Tom. Ignorez Tom.
```

(I'm not sure what `Tom` did to the author of the dataset...)

There are often rows with duplicate French translations for each English translation. This occurs when there are multiple common ways to translate the English phrase. Have a look at the following code for example:

```
Go now.     Va, maintenant.
Go now.     Allez-y maintenant.
Go now.     Vas-y maintenant.
```

Since we are building a character-level sequence-to-sequence model, we will need to load the data into memory and then one hot encode each input and output saying at the character level. That's the hard part. Let's do that next.

Loading data

There is quite a bit involved with loading this data. You might want to refer to the code block as you read though this text.

The first for loop in the code below is going to loop through the entire input file or some number of samples that we specify when we call `load_data()`. I'm doing this because you might not have the RAM to load the entire dataset. You might get good results with as few as 10,000 examples; however, more is always better.

As we loop through the input file, line by line, we're doing several things at once:

- We're wrapping each French translation in a `'\t'` to start the phrase and a `'\n'` to end it. This corresponds to the <SOS> and <EOS> tags I used in the sequence-to-sequence diagram. This will allow us to use `'\t'` as an input to seed the decoder when we want to generate a translation sequence.
- We are splitting each line into the English input, and its respective French translation. These are stored in the lists `input_texts` and `target_texts`.
- Finally, we are adding each character of both the input and target text into a set. Those sets are called `input_characters` and `target_characters`. We will use these sets when it's time to one hot encode our phrases.

After our loop completes, we will convert the character sets into sorted lists. We will also create variables called `num_encoder_tokens` and `num_decoder_tokens` to hold the size of each of these lists. We will need these later for one hot encoding as well.

In order to get the inputs and targets into a matrix, we will need to pad the phrases to the length of the longest phrase, just as we did in the last chapter. To do that, we will need to know the longest phrase. We will store that in `max_encoder_seq_length` and `max_decoder_seq_length`, as shown in the following code:

```
def load_data(num_samples=50000, start_char='\t', end_char='\n',
data_path='data/fra-eng/fra.txt'):
    input_texts = []
    target_texts = []
    input_characters = set()
    target_characters = set()
    lines = open(data_path, 'r', encoding='utf-8').read().split('\n')
    for line in lines[: min(num_samples, len(lines) - 1)]:
        input_text, target_text = line.split('\t')
        target_text = start_char + target_text + end_char
        input_texts.append(input_text)
        target_texts.append(target_text)
        for char in input_text:
            if char not in input_characters:
                input_characters.add(char)
        for char in target_text:
            if char not in target_characters:
                target_characters.add(char)
```

```
input_characters = sorted(list(input_characters))
target_characters = sorted(list(target_characters))
num_encoder_tokens = len(input_characters)
num_decoder_tokens = len(target_characters)
max_encoder_seq_length = max([len(txt) for txt in input_texts])
max_decoder_seq_length = max([len(txt) for txt in target_texts])

print('Number of samples:', len(input_texts))
print('Number of unique input tokens:', num_encoder_tokens)
print('Number of unique output tokens:', num_decoder_tokens)
print('Max sequence length for inputs:', max_encoder_seq_length)
print('Max sequence length for outputs:', max_decoder_seq_length)
return {'input_texts': input_texts, 'target_texts': target_texts,
        'input_chars': input_characters, 'target_chars':
        target_characters, 'num_encoder_tokens': num_encoder_tokens,
        'num_decoder_tokens': num_decoder_tokens,
        'max_encoder_seq_length': max_encoder_seq_length,
        'max_decoder_seq_length': max_decoder_seq_length}
```

After our data is loaded, we will return all this information in a dictionary that can be passed along to a function that will one hot encode each phrase. Let's do that next.

One hot encoding

In this function, we will be taking the dictionary we just built and one hot encoding the text of each phrase.

Once we're done, we will be left with three dictionaries. Each of them will be of dimension [*number of texts * max sequence length * tokens*]. If you squint, and think back to the simpler times of `Chapter 10`, *Training LSTMs with Word Embeddings from Scratch,* you can see this is really the same as the other NLP models we've done on the input side. We will define one hot encoding using the following code:

```
def one_hot_vectorize(data):
    input_chars = data['input_chars']
    target_chars = data['target_chars']
    input_texts = data['input_texts']
    target_texts = data['target_texts']
    max_encoder_seq_length = data['max_encoder_seq_length']
    max_decoder_seq_length = data['max_decoder_seq_length']
    num_encoder_tokens = data['num_encoder_tokens']
    num_decoder_tokens = data['num_decoder_tokens']

    input_token_index = dict([(char, i) for i, char in
      enumerate(input_chars)])
```

```
target_token_index = dict([(char, i) for i, char in
  enumerate(target_chars)])
encoder_input_data = np.zeros((len(input_texts),
  max_encoder_seq_length, num_encoder_tokens), dtype='float32')
decoder_input_data = np.zeros((len(input_texts),
  max_decoder_seq_length, num_decoder_tokens), dtype='float32')
decoder_target_data = np.zeros((len(input_texts),
  max_decoder_seq_length, num_decoder_tokens), dtype='float32')

for i, (input_text, target_text) in enumerate(zip(input_texts,
  target_texts)):
    for t, char in enumerate(input_text):
        encoder_input_data[i, t, input_token_index[char]] = 1.
    for t, char in enumerate(target_text):
# decoder_target_data is ahead of decoder_input_data by one
  timestep
        decoder_input_data[i, t, target_token_index[char]] = 1.
        if t > 0:
        # decoder_target_data will be ahead by one timestep
        # and will not include the start character.
        decoder_target_data[i, t - 1, target_token_index[char]] = 1.
data['input_token_index'] = input_token_index
data['target_token_index'] = target_token_index
data['encoder_input_data'] = encoder_input_data
data['decoder_input_data'] = decoder_input_data
data['decoder_target_data'] = decoder_target_data
return data
```

There are three training vectors that we create in this code. Before moving on, I want to make sure we understand each of these vectors:

- `encoder_input_data` is a 3D matrix of shape (`number_of_pairs, max_english_sequence_length, number_of_english_characters`).
- `decoder_input_data` is a 3d matrix of shape (`number_of_pairs, max_french_sequence_length, number_of_french_characters`).
- `decoder_output_data` is the same as `decoder_input_data` shifted one time step ahead. This means that `decoder_input_data[:, t+1, :]` is equal to `decoder_output_data[:, t, :]`.

Each of the preceding vectors is a one hot encoded representation of an entire phrase at the character level. This means that if our input phrase was Go! The first time step of the vector would contain an element for every possible English character in the text. Each of these elements would be set to 0, except g, which would be set to 1.

Our goal will be to train a sequence-to-sequence model to predict `decoder_output_data` using `encoder_input_data` and `decoder_input` data as our input features.

And at long last our data prep is done, so we can start to build our sequence-to-sequence network architecture.

Training network architecture

In this example, we're actually going to use two separate architectures, one for training and one for inference. We will use the trained layers from training in the inference model. While really we're using the same parts for each architecture, to make things more clear I will show each part separately. The following is the model we will use to train the network:

```
encoder_input = Input(shape=(None, num_encoder_tokens),
name='encoder_input')
encoder_outputs, state_h, state_c = LSTM(lstm_units, return_state=True,
name="encoder_lstm")(encoder_input)
encoder_states = [state_h, state_c]
decoder_input = Input(shape=(None, num_decoder_tokens),
name='decoder_input')
decoder_lstm = LSTM(lstm_units, return_sequences=True,
   return_state=True, name="decoder_lstm")
decoder_outputs, _, _ = decoder_lstm(decoder_input,
initial_state=encoder_states)
decoder_dense = Dense(num_decoder_tokens, activation='softmax',
   name='softmax_output')
decoder_output = decoder_dense(decoder_outputs)

model = Model([encoder_input, decoder_input], decoder_output)
model.compile(optimizer='rmsprop', loss='categorical_crossentropy')
```

If we *zoom into* the encoder, we see a fairly standard LSTM. What's different is that we're getting the states from the encoder (`return_state=True`), which we don't typically do if we're connecting an LSTM to a dense layer. These states are what we will capture in `encoder_states`. We will use them to provide context to, or condition, the decoder.

On the decoder side, we're setting up `decoder_lstm` slightly different from how we have previously constructed a Keras layer, but it's really just slightly different syntax.

Have a look at the following code:

```
decoder_lstm = LSTM(lstm_units, return_sequences=True,
   return_state=True, name="decoder_lstm")
decoder_outputs, _, _ = decoder_lstm(decoder_input,
```

```
initial_state=encoder_states)
```

Its functionally the same as the following code:

```
decoder_outputs, _, _ = LSTM(lstm_units, return_sequences=True,
    return_state=True, name="decoder_lstm")(decoder_input,
initial_state=encoder_states)
```

The reason why I did this will become apparent in the inference architecture.

Please note that the the decoder takes the encoder's hidden states as its initial state. The decoder output is then passed to a `softmax` layer that predicts `decoder_output_data`.

Lastly, we will define our training model, which I will creatively call `model`, as one that takes `encoder_input_data` and `decoder_input` data as inputs and predicts `decoder_output_data`.

Network architecture (for inference)

In order to predict an entire sequence given an input sequence, we need to rearrange our architecture just a little. I suspect in future versions of Keras this will be made simpler, but it's a necessary step as of today.

Why does it need to be different? Because we won't have the `decoder_input_data` teacher vector on inference. We're on our own now. So, we will have to set things up so that we don't require that vector.

Let's take a look at this inference architecture, and then step through the code:

```
encoder_model = Model(encoder_input, encoder_states)

decoder_state_input_h = Input(shape=(lstm_units,))
decoder_state_input_c = Input(shape=(lstm_units,))
decoder_states_inputs = [decoder_state_input_h, decoder_state_input_c]
decoder_outputs, state_h, state_c = decoder_lstm(
    decoder_input, initial_state=decoder_states_inputs)
decoder_states = [state_h, state_c]
decoder_outputs = decoder_dense(decoder_outputs)
decoder_model = Model(
    [decoder_input] + decoder_states_inputs,
    [decoder_outputs] + decoder_states)
```

First, we start off by building an encoder model. This model will take an input sequence and return the hidden states of the LSTM we trained in the previous model.

The decoder model then has two inputs, the h and c hidden states that condition its output, derived from the encoder model. Collectively, we call these `decoder_states_inputs`.

We can reuse `decoder_lstm` from above; however, this time we aren't going to discard the states, `state_h` and `state_c`. We're going to instead pass them as network outputs, along with the `softmax` prediction of the target.

Now, when we infer a new output sequence, we can get these states after the first character is predicted and pass them back into the LSTM with the `softmax` predictions so that the LSTM can predict another character. We will repeat that loop until the decoder generates a `'\n'` which signals we've reach the <EOS>.

We will look at the inference code shortly; for now, let's look at how we train and serialize this collection of models.

Putting it all together

As is tradition in this book, I will show you how the entire architecture for this model fits together here:

```python
def build_models(lstm_units, num_encoder_tokens, num_decoder_tokens):
    # train model
    encoder_input = Input(shape=(None, num_encoder_tokens),
        name='encoder_input')
    encoder_outputs, state_h, state_c = LSTM(lstm_units,
        return_state=True, name="encoder_lstm")(encoder_input)
    encoder_states = [state_h, state_c]
    decoder_input = Input(shape=(None, num_decoder_tokens),
        name='decoder_input')
    decoder_lstm = LSTM(lstm_units, return_sequences=True,
        return_state=True, name="decoder_lstm")
    decoder_outputs, _, _ = decoder_lstm(decoder_input,
                                    initial_state=encoder_states)
    decoder_dense = Dense(num_decoder_tokens, activation='softmax',
                    name='softmax_output')
    decoder_output = decoder_dense(decoder_outputs)
    model = Model([encoder_input, decoder_input], decoder_output)
    model.compile(optimizer='rmsprop', loss='categorical_crossentropy')

    encoder_model = Model(encoder_input, encoder_states)
    decoder_state_input_h = Input(shape=(lstm_units,))
    decoder_state_input_c = Input(shape=(lstm_units,))
    decoder_states_inputs = [decoder_state_input_h,
        decoder_state_input_c]
```

```
decoder_outputs, state_h, state_c = decoder_lstm(
    decoder_input, initial_state=decoder_states_inputs)
decoder_states = [state_h, state_c]
decoder_outputs = decoder_dense(decoder_outputs)
decoder_model = Model(
    [decoder_input] + decoder_states_inputs,
    [decoder_outputs] + decoder_states)

return model, encoder_model, decoder_model
```

Note that we are returning all three models here. After the training model is trained, I will serialize all three with the `keras model.save()` method.

Training

We're finally ready to train our sequence-to-sequence network. The following code makes calls to all our data loading functions first, creates our callbacks, and then fits the model:

```
data = load_data()
data = one_hot_vectorize(data)
callbacks = create_callbacks("char_s2s")
model, encoder_model, decoder_model = build_models(256,
data['num_encoder_tokens'], data['num_decoder_tokens'])
print(model.summary())

model.fit(x=[data["encoder_input_data"], data["decoder_input_data"]],
          y=data["decoder_target_data"],
          batch_size=64,
          epochs=100,
          validation_split=0.2,
          callbacks=callbacks)

model.save('char_s2s_train.h5')
encoder_model.save('char_s2s_encoder.h5')
decoder_model.save('char_s2s_decoder.h5')
```

You'll note that I previously haven't defined a validation or test set like we normally do. This time, following the example set forth in the blog post, I'll let Keras randomly choose 20% of the data as validation, which works perfectly fine in an example. If you're going to use this code to actually do machine translation, please use a separate test set.

After the training model is fit, I'm going to save all three models and load them again in a separate program built for inference. I'm doing this to keep the code somewhat clean because the inference code is quite complex in itself.

Lets take a look at 100 epochs of model training for this model:

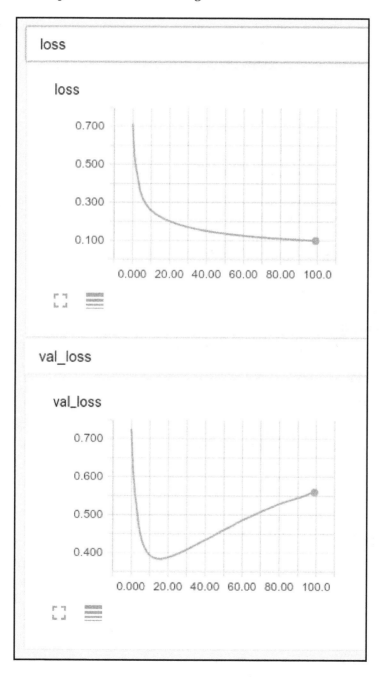

As you can see, we start to overfit somewhere around epoch 20. While loss continues to decrease, `val_loss` is increasing. Model check pointing is probably going to work less than well in this scenario, since we won't be serializing the inference model until after training is over. So, ideally, we should train one more time, setting the number of epochs we train for to just slightly more than the smallest value observed in TensorBoard.

Inference

Now that we have a trained model, we're going to actually generate some translations.

Overall, the steps for inference are as follows:

1. Load the data and vectorize again (we need the character to index mappings and a few translations to test with)
2. Using the character to index dictionaries, we will create reverse index to character dictionaries, so we can get back from numbers to characters once we predict the proper character
3. Pick some input sequence to translate, then run it through the encoder, obtaining the states
4. Send the states and the <SOS> character, '\t', to the decoder.
5. Loop, getting each next character, until the decoder generates an <EOS> or '\n'

Loading data

We can just import the `load_data` and `one_hot_vectorize` functions from the training script, calling those methods the same way, as shown in the following code:

```
data = load_data()
data = one_hot_vectorize(data)
```

Creating reverse indices

The decoder is going to predict the index of the correct character, which will be the `argmax` of the `softmax` output of the decoder. We're going to need to be able to map the index to the character. As you might recall, we have a character to index mapping already in the data dictionary, so we just need to reverse it. It's simple enough to reverse a dictionary, as follows:

```
def create_reverse_indicies(data):
```

```
data['reverse_target_char_index'] = dict(
    (i, char) for char, i in data["target_token_index"].items())
return data
```

Then, we can call this function as follows:

```
data = create_reverse_indicies(data)
```

Loading models

We can load the models we saved in the training script with `keras.models.load_model`. I created this helper to do just that. We will load the model using the following code:

```
def load_models():
    model = load_model('char_s2s.h5')
    encoder_model = load_model('char_s2s_encoder.h5')
    decoder_model = load_model('char_s2s_decoder.h5')
    return [model, encoder_model, decoder_model]
```

We can just call the following function to load all the three models:

```
model, encoder_model, decoder_model = load_models()
```

Translating a sequence

Now we're ready to sample a few input sequences and translate them. In the example code, we're using the first 100 bilingual pairs to translate with. A better test might be to sample randomly across the space, but I think this simple loop illustrates the process:

```
for seq_index in range(100):
    input_seq = data["encoder_input_data"][seq_index: seq_index + 1]
    decoded_sentence = decode_sequence(input_seq, data, encoder_model,
                                       decoder_model)
    print('-')
    print('Input sentence:', data['input_texts'][seq_index])
    print('Correct Translation:', data['target_texts']
        [seq_index].strip("\t\n"))
    print('Decoded sentence:', decoded_sentence)
```

In this code, we're using one observation of `encoder_input_data` as the input to `decode_sequence`. `decode_sequence` will pass back the sequence that the decoder believes is the correct translation. We also need to pass it the encoder and decoder models so it can do its job.The translation following is more interesting because the learned phrase isn't connected to

Once we have the decoder prediction, we can compare it to the input and the correct translation.

Of course, we aren't quite done because we haven't explored how the `decode_sequence` method works. That's next.

Decoding a sequence

The decoder needs the following two things to start its work:

- State from the encoder.
- An input signal that starts the predicted translation. We will send it a `'\t'` in a one hot vector as that's our `<SOS>` character.

To obtain the encoder state, we just need to send the vectorized version of the phrase we want to translate to the encoder, using the following code:

```
states_value = encoder_model.predict(input_seq)
```

In order to start the decoder, we also need a one hot vector containing the `<SOS>` character. This code gets us there:

```
target_seq = np.zeros((1, 1, data['num_decoder_tokens']))
target_seq[0, 0, data['target_token_index']['\t']] = 1.
```

And now we're ready to set up a decoder loop that will generate our translated phrase, using the following code:

```
stop_condition = False
decoded_sentence = ''
while not stop_condition:
    output_tokens, h, c = decoder_model.predict(
        [target_seq] + states_value)

    sampled_token_index = np.argmax(output_tokens[0, -1, :])
    sampled_char = data["reverse_target_char_index"][sampled_token_index]
    decoded_sentence += sampled_char

    if (sampled_char == '\n' or
       len(decoded_sentence) > data['max_decoder_seq_length']):
        stop_condition = True

    target_seq = np.zeros((1, 1, data['num_decoder_tokens']))
    target_seq[0, 0, sampled_token_index] = 1.
```

```
states_value = [h, c]
```

The first thing to notice is that we're looping until `stop_condition = True`. This occurs when the decoder generates a `'\n'`.

The first pass through the loop I call the predict method of the `decoder_model` using the `<SOS>` vector and the states from the encoder that we created outside of the loop.

Of course, `output_tokens` will contain the `softmax` predictions of each character the decoder can predict. By taking the `argmax` of `output_tokens`, we will get the index of the largest `softmax` value. Conveniently, I can convert that back into the associated character with the `reverse_target_char_index` I created before, a dictionary that converts between indices and characters.

Next, we will append that character to the `decode_sequence` string.

Following that, we can check whether that character is a `'\n'` triggering `stop_condition` to be `True`.

Lastly, we will create a new `target_seq` containing the last character the decoder generated and a list containing the hidden states of the decoder. Now we're ready to repeat the loop again.

Our decoder just follows this process until the decoded sequence has been generated.

Example translations

Just for fun, I've provided a few attempted translations here. These all come from the front of the training set, which means I'm making predictions on the `training` dataset, so these translations likely make the model look better than it actually is.

Our first translation gives you a feel for what we're expecting, and the network does a good job:

Input sentence: Help!

Correct translation: *À l'aide!*

Decoded sentence: *À l'aide!*

The translation following is more interesting because the learned phrase isn't connected to any of the training phrases. The phrase *Vas-tu immédiatement!* translates to something like *You go immediately* which is very similar and perhaps even correct:

Input sentence: *Go on.*
Correct translation: *Poursuis.*
Decoded sentence: *Vas-tu immédiatement!*

-

Input sentence: *Go on.*
Correct translation: *Continuez.*
Decoded sentence: *Vas-tu immédiatement!*

-

Input sentence: *Go on.*
Correct translation: *Poursuivez.*
Decoded sentence: *Vas-tu immédiatement!*

-

Of course, there are many ways to say the same thing, which makes things more difficult for the network:

Input sentence: *Come on!*
Correct translation: *Allez !*
Decoded sentence: *Allez!*

-

Input sentence: *Come on.*
Correct translation: *Allez!*
Decoded sentence: *Allez!*

-

Input sentence: *Come on.*
Correct translation: *Viens!*
Decoded sentence: *Allez!*

-

Input sentence: *Come on.*
Correct translation: *Venez!*
Decoded sentence: *Allez!*

Summary

In this chapter, we covered the basics of sequence-to-sequence models, including how they work and how we can use them. Hopefully, we've shown you a powerful tool for machine translation, question-answering, and chat applications.

If you've made it this far, good job. You've seen quite a few applications of deep learning and you're finding yourself on the right of the bell curve toward the state-of-the-art in the application of deep neural networks.

In the next chapter, I'm going to show you an example of another advanced topic, deep reinforcement learning, or deep-Q learning, and show you how to implement your own deep-Q network.

Until then, *sois détendu*!

12
Using Deep Reinforcement Learning

In this chapter, we're going to be using deep neural networks in a slightly different way. Rather than predicting the membership of a class, estimating a value, or even generating a sequence, we're going to be building an intelligent agent. While the terms machine learning and artificial intelligence are often used interchangeably, in this chapter we will talk about an artificial intelligence as an intelligent agent that can perceive it's environment, and take steps to accomplish some goal in that environment.

Imagine an agent that can play a strategy game such as Chess or Go. A very naive approach to building a neural network to solve such a game might be to use a network architecture where we one hot encode every possible board/piece combination and then predict every possible next move. As massive and complex as that network would be, it probably wouldn't do a very good job. To play Chess well, you have to consider not only your next move, but the moves that follow. Our intelligent agent is going to need to consider the optimal next move given future moves, in a non-deterministic world.

This is an exciting field. It's in this domain of intelligent agents that researchers are making progress towards artificial general intelligence or strong AI, which is the lofty goal of creating intelligent agents that can perform any intellectual task that a human can. This notion of strong AI is typically contrasted with weak AI, which is the ability to solve some single task or application.

This chapter is going to be a challenge for both the author (me) and the readers (you) because reinforcement learning deserves it's own book and needs to summarize work done on math, psychology, and computer science. As such, please forgive the quick reference treatment and know that I'm attempting to give you exactly enough and not a drop more in the coming sections.

Reinforcement learning, Markov Decision Processes, and Q-learning are the building blocks to an intelligent agent, and we will talk about those next.

We will discuss the following topics in this chapter:

- Reinforcement learning overview
- Keras reinforcement learning framework
- Building a reinforcement learning agent in Keras

Reinforcement learning overview

Reinforcement learning is based on the concept of an intelligent agent. An agent interacts with it's environment by observing some state and then taking an action. As the agent takes actions to move between states, it receives feedback about the goodness of its actions in the form of a reward signal. This reward signal is the reinforcement in reinforcement learning. It's a feedback loop that the agent can use to learn the goodness of it's choice. Of course, rewards can be both positive and negative (punishments).

Imagine a self-driving car as the agent we are building. As it's driving down the road, it's receiving a constant stream of reward signals for it's actions. Staying within the lanes would likely lead to a positive reward while running over pedestrians would likely result in a very negative reward for the agent. When faced with the choice of staying in the lines, or hitting a pedestrian, the agent will hopefully learn to avoid the pedestrian at the expense of swerving outside the lines, losing lane line reward in order to avoid a much greater pedestrian collision punishment.

Central to the idea of reinforcement learning are the concepts of state, action, and reward. I've already discussed reward, so lets' talk about action and state. Action is what the agent can do, when it observes some state. If our agent were playing a simple board game, the action would be the thing that the agent does on it's turn. The turn is then the agent's state. For the sake of the problems we will be looking at here, the actions an agent can take are always finite and discrete. This concept is illustrated in the following figure:

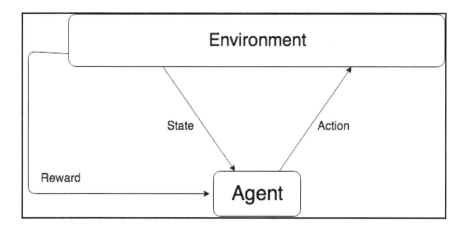

One step of this feedback loop can be expressed mathematically as follows:

$$s \xrightarrow{a} r, s'$$

Actions transition the agent between it's original state s and it's next state s', where the it receives some reward r. The way the agent chooses actions is called the **agent's policy** and it is typically noted as π.

The goal of reinforcement learning is to find a sequence of actions that get the agent from state to state with as much reward as possible.

Markov Decision Processes

This world that we've framed up happens to be a **Markov Decision Process** (**MDP**), which has the following properties:

- It has a finite set of states, S
- It has a finite set of actions, A
- $P_a(s, s')$ is the probability that taking action A will transition between state s and state s'
- $R_a(s, s')$ is the immediate reward for transition between s and s'
- $\gamma \in [0, 1]$ is the discount factor, which is how much we discount future rewards over present rewards (more on this later)

Once we have a policy function π that determines which action to take for each state, the MDP has been solved and becomes a Markov chain.

And good news, it's totally possible to solve an MDP perfectly, with one caveat. That caveat is that all the rewards and probabilities for the MDP have to be known. It turns out this caveat is rather important because most of the time an agent can't know all the rewards and state change probabilities because the agent's environment is chaotic, or at least non-deterministic.

Q Learning

Imagine that we have some function, Q, that can estimate the reward for taking an action:

$$r = Q(s, a)$$

For some state s, and action a, it generates a reward for that action given the state. If we knew all the rewards for our environment, we could just loop through Q and pick the action that gives us the biggest reward. But, as we mentioned in the previous section, our agent can't know all the reward states and state probabilities. So, then our Q function needs to attempt to approximate the reward.

We can approximate this ideal Q function with a recursively defined Q function called the **Bellman Equation**:

$$Q(s, a) = r_0 + \gamma \, max_a \, Q(s', a)$$

In this case, r_0 is the reward for the next action and then we use the Q function recursively on the next action (over and over recursively) to determine the future reward for the action. In doing so, we apply gamma γ as a discount to future rewards relative to current rewards. As long as gamma is less than 1, it keeps our reward series from being infinite. More obviously, a reward in the future state is less less valuable than the same reward in the current state. Concretely, if someone offered you $100 today, or $100 tomorrow, you should take the money now because tomorrow is uncertain.

If we did our best to allow our agent to experience every possible state transition, and used this function to estimate our reward, we would arrive at that ideal Q function we were trying to approximate.

Infinite state space

This discussion of Q functions brings us to an important limitation of traditional reinforcement learning. As you may recall, it assumes a finite and discrete set of state spaces. Unfortunately that isn't the world we live in, nor is it the environment that our agents will find themselves in much of the time. Consider an agent that can play ping pong. One important part of it's state space would be the velocity of the ping pong ball, which is certainly not discrete. An agent that can see, like one we will cover shortly, would be presented with an image, that is a large continuous space.

The Bellman equation we discussed would require us to keep a big matrix of experienced rewards as we moved from state to state. But, when faced with a continuous state space this isn't possible. The possible states are essentially infinite and we can't create a matrix of infinite size.

Luckily for us, we can use a deep neural network to approximate the Q function. This probably doesn't surprise you because you're reading a deep learning book, so you probably guessed deep learning had to come into the picture someplace. This is that place.

Deep Q networks

Deep Q networks (DQNs) are neural networks that approximate the Q function. They map states to actions and they learn to estimate the Q value of each action, as shown in the following figure:

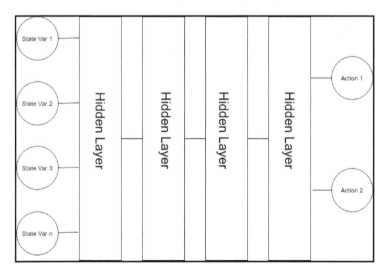

Instead of trying to store a matrix that's infinitely large, mapping the rewards from continuous state spaces to actions, we can use a deep neural network as a function to approximate that matrix. In this way, we can use a neural network as the brain of an intelligent agent. But this all leads us to a very interesting question. How do we train this network?

Online learning

As our agent transitions from state to state, by taking actions, it receives a reward. The agent can learn online by using each state, action, and reward as training input. After every action, the agent will update it's neural network weights, hopefully getting smarter along the way. This is the basic idea of online learning. The agent learns as it goes, just like you and I do.

The shortcomings of this naive type of online learning are somewhat obvious and two-fold:

- We throw away our experience after we experience it.
- The experiences we work through are highly correlated to each other and we will overfit to the most recent experiences. Interestingly enough, this is something humans suffer from too, called availability bias.

We can solve these problems by using memory and experience replay.

Memory and experience replay

A clever solution to these two problems is available when we introduce the concept of a finite memory space where we store a set of experiences the agent has had. At each state, we can take the opportunity to remember the state, action and reward. Then, periodically, the agent can replay these experiences by sampling a random minibatch from memory and updating the DQN weights using that minibatch.

This replay mechanism allows the agent to learn from it's experiences in the longer term, in a general way, since it's sampling from those experiences in it's memory randomly rather than updating the entire network using just the last experience.

Exploitation versus exploration

Generally, we want the agent to follow a *greedy* policy, which means we want the agent to take the action that has the biggest Q value. While the network is learning, we don't want it to always behave greedily, however. If it did so, it would never explore new options, and learn new things. So, we need our agent to occasionally operate off policy.

The best way to balance this exploration is an ongoing research topic and it has been used for a very long time. The method we will be using, however, is pretty straightforward. Every time the agent takes an action, we will generate a random number. If that number is equal to or less than some threshold ϵ then the agent will take a random action. This is called an **ϵ-greedy policy**.

When the agent first starts, it doesn't know much about the world and it should probably explore more. As the agent gets smarter, it should probably explore less and use it's knowledge of the environment more. To do so, we just need to gradually decrease ϵ as we train. In our example, we will decrease epsilon by a decay rate every turn, so that it decreases linearly with each action.

Putting this together, we have a **linear annealed ϵ-greedy Q policy**, which is both simple and fun to say.

DeepMind

No discussion of reinforcement learning would be complete without at least a mention of the paper, *Playing Atari with Deep Reinforcement Learning* by Mnih et al. (https://www.cs.toronto.edu/~vmnih/docs/dqn.pdf) then of DeepMind, now of Google. In this landmark paper, the authors used a convolutional neural network to train a deep Q network to play Atari 2600 games. They took the raw pixel output from the Atari 2600 games, scaled it down a bit, converted it to gray scale, and then used that as the state space input for the network. In order for the computer to understand the velocity and direction of the objects on screen, they used a four image buffer as an input to the deep Q network.

The authors were able to create an agent that was able to play seven Atari 2600 games with the exact same neural network architecture, and the agent was better than a human on three of those games. This was later extended to 49 games, the majority of which it was better at than a human. This paper was a really important step towards general AI, and it's really the foundation of much of the research currently happening in reinforcement learning.

The Keras reinforcement learning framework

At this point, we should have just enough background to start building a deep Q network, but there's still a pretty big hurdle we need to overcome.

Implementing an agent that utilizes deep reinforcement learning can be quite a challenge, however the Keras-RL library originally authored by Matthias Plappert makes it much easier. I'll be using his library to power the agents presented in this chapter.

Of course, our agent can't have much fun without an environment. I'll be using the OpenAI gym, which provides many environments, complete with states and reward functions, that we can easily use to build worlds for our agents to explore.

Installing Keras-RL

Keras-RL can be installed by pip. However, I recommend installing it from the project GitHub repo, as the code might be slightly newer. To do so, simply clone the repo and run `python setup.py install` as follows:

```
git clone https://github.com/matthiasplappert/keras-rl.git
cd keras-rl
python setup.py install
```

Installing OpenAI gym

The OpenAI gym is available as a pip install. I'll be using examples from their `Box2D` and `atari` environments. You can install these using the following code:

```
pip install gym
pip install gym[atari]
pip install gym[Box2D]
```

Using OpenAI gym

Using the OpenAI gym really makes deep reinforcement learning easy. Keras-RL will do most of the hard work, but I think it's worth walking through the gym separately so that you can understand how the agent interacts with the environment.

Environments are objects that can be instantiated. For example, to create a `CartPole-v0` environment, we just need to import the gym and create the environment, as shown in the following code:

```
import gym
env = gym.make("CartPole-v0")
```

Now, if our agent wants to act in that environment, it just needs to send an `action` and get back a state and a `reward`, as follows:

```
next_state, reward, done, info = env.step(action)
```

The agent can play through an entire episode by using a loop to interact with the environment. Every iteration of this loop corresponds to a single step in the episode. The episode is over when the agent receives a 'done' signal from the environment.

Building a reinforcement learning agent in Keras

Good news, we're finally ready to start coding. In this section, I'm going to demonstrate two Keras-RL agents called **CartPole** and **Lunar Lander**. I've chosen these examples because they won't consume your GPU and your cloud budget to run. They can be easily extended to Atari problems, and I've included one of those as well in the book's Git repository. You can find all this code in the `Chapter12` folder, as usual. Let's talk quickly about these two environments:

- **CartPole**: The CartPole environment consists of a pole, balanced on a cart. The agent has to learn how to balance the pole vertically, while the cart underneath it moves. The agent is given the position of the cart, the velocity of the cart, the angle of the pole, and the rotational rate of the pole as inputs. The agent can apply a force on either side of the cart. If the pole falls more than 15 degrees from vertical, it's game over for our agent.

- **Lunar Lander**: The Lunar Lander environment is quite a bit more challenging. The agent has to land a lunar lander on a landing pad. The surface of the moon changes, as does the orientation of the lander every episode. The agent is given an eight-dimensional array describing the state of the world in each step and can take one of four actions in that step. The agent can choose to do nothing, fire its main engine, fire it's left orientation engine, or fire it's right orientation engine.

CartPole

The CartPole agent will use a fairly modest neural network that you should be able to train fairly quickly even without a GPU. We will start by looking at the model architecture as always. Then we will define the network's memory, exploration policy, and finally train the agent.

CartPole neural network architecture

Three hidden layers with 16 neurons each is really probably more than enough to solve this simple problem. This model closely resembles some of the basic models we used in the beginning of the book. We will use the following code to define the model:

```
def build_model(state_size, num_actions):
    input = Input(shape=(1,state_size))
    x = Flatten()(input)
    x = Dense(16, activation='relu')(x)
    x = Dense(16, activation='relu')(x)
    x = Dense(16, activation='relu')(x)
    output = Dense(num_actions, activation='linear')(x)
    model = Model(inputs=input, outputs=output)
    print(model.summary())
    return model
```

The input will be a 1 x state space vector and there will be an output neuron for each possible action that will predict the Q value of that action for each step. By taking the `argmax` of the outputs, we can choose the action with the highest *Q* value, but we don't have to do that ourselves as Keras-RL will do it for us.

Memory

Keras-RL provides us with a class called `rl.memory.SequentialMemory` that provides a fast and efficient data structure that we can store the agent's experiences in:

```
memory = SequentialMemory(limit=50000, window_length=1)
```

We need to specify a maximum size for this memory object, which is a hyperparameter. As new experiences are added to this memory and it becomes full, old experiences are forgotten.

Policy

Keras-RL provides an ∈-greedy Q Policy called `rl.policy.EpsGreedyQPolicy` that we can use to balance exploration and exploitation. We can use `rl.policy.LinearAnnealedPolicy` to decay our ∈ as the agent steps forward in the world, as shown in the following code:

```
policy = LinearAnnealedPolicy(EpsGreedyQPolicy(), attr='eps', value_max=1.,
value_min=.1, value_test=.05, nb_steps=10000)
```

Here we're saying that we want to start with a value of 1 for ∈ and go no smaller than 0.1, while testing if our random number is less than 0.05. We set the number of steps between 1 and .1 to 10,000 and Keras-RL handles the decay math for us.

Agent

With a model, memory, and policy defined, we're now ready to create a deep Q network Agent and send that agent those objects. Keras RL provides an agent class called `rl.agents.dqn.DQNAgent` that we can use for this, as shown in the following code:

```
dqn = DQNAgent(model=model, nb_actions=num_actions, memory=memory,
nb_steps_warmup=10,
                target_model_update=1e-2, policy=policy)

dqn.compile(Adam(lr=1e-3), metrics=['mae'])
```

Two of these parameters are probably unfamiliar at this point, `target_model_update` and `nb_steps_warmup`:

- `nb_steps_warmup`: Determines how long we wait before we start doing experience replay, which if you recall, is when we actually start training the network. This lets us build up enough experience to build a proper minibatch. If you choose a value for this parameter that's smaller than your batch size, Keras RL will sample with a replacement.

- `target_model_update`: The Q function is recursive and when the agent updates it's network for Q(s,a) that update also impacts the prediction it will make for Q(s', a). This can make for a very unstable network. The way most deep Q network implementations address this limitation is by using a target network, which is a copy of the deep Q network that isn't trained, but rather replaced with a fresh copy every so often. The `target_model_update` parameter controls how often this happens.

Training

Keras RL provides several Keras-like callbacks that allow for convenient model check pointing and logging. I'll use both of those callbacks below. If you would like to see more of the callbacks Keras-RL provides, they can be found here: `https://github.com/matthiasplappert/keras-rl/blob/master/rl/callbacks.py`. You can also find a Callback class that you can use to create your own Keras-RL callbacks.

We will use the following code to train our model:

```
def build_callbacks(env_name):
    checkpoint_weights_filename = 'dqn_' + env_name + '_weights_{step}.h5f'
    log_filename = 'dqn_{}_log.json'.format(env_name)
    callbacks = [ModelIntervalCheckpoint(checkpoint_weights_filename,
interval=5000)]
    callbacks += [FileLogger(log_filename, interval=100)]
    return callbacks

callbacks = build_callbacks(ENV_NAME)

dqn.fit(env, nb_steps=50000,
 visualize=False,
 verbose=2,
 callbacks=callbacks)
```

Once the agent's callbacks are built, we can fit the `DQNAgent` as we would a Keras model, by using a `.fit()` method. Take note of the `visualize` parameter in this example. If `visualize` were set to `True`, we would be able to watch the agent interact with the environment as we went. However, this significantly slows down the training.

Results

After the first 250 episodes, we will see that the total rewards for the episode approach 200 and the episode steps also approach 200. This means that the agent has learned to balance the pole on the cart until the environment ends at a maximum of 200 steps.

It's of course fun to watch our success, so we can use the DQNAgent .test() method to evaluate for some number of episodes. The following code is used to define this method:

```
dqn.test(env, nb_episodes=5, visualize=True)
```

Here we've set visualize=True so we can watch our agent balance the pole, as shown in the following image:

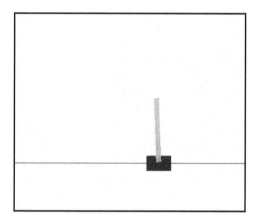

There we go, that's one balanced pole! Alright, I know, I'll admit that balancing a pole on a cart isn't all that cool, so let's do one more lightweight example. In this example, we will land a lunar lander on the moon, which will hopefully impress you more.

Lunar Lander

The agent we use for Lunar Lander will be almost identical to CartPole, with the exception of the actual model architecture and a few hyperparameter changes, thanks to Keras-RL. The environment for Lunar Lander has eight inputs instead of four and our agent can now choose four actions instead of two.

If you're inspired by these examples and decide to try your hand at building a Keras-RL network, keep in mind that hyperparameter choice is very, very important. In the case of the Lunar Lander agent, the smallest changes to the model architecture caused my agent to to fail to learn a solution to the environment. Getting the network just right is hard work.

Lunar Lander network architecture

The architecture for my Lunar Lander agent is only slightly more complicated than for CartPole, introducing just a few more neurons for the same three hidden layers. We will use the following code to define the model:

```
def build_model(state_size, num_actions):
    input = Input(shape=(1, state_size))
    x = Flatten()(input)
    x = Dense(64, activation='relu')(x)
    x = Dense(32, activation='relu')(x)
    x = Dense(16, activation='relu')(x)
    output = Dense(num_actions, activation='linear')(x)
    model = Model(inputs=input, outputs=output)
    print(model.summary())
    return model
```

In the case of this problem, smaller architectures resulted in an agent that learned to control and hover the lander, but not actually land it. Of course, because we're making minibatch updates for every step in every episode, we need to carefully weigh complexity against runtime and computational needs.

Memory and policy

The memory and policy from CartPole can be reused. I believe it might be possible to improve the speed of agent training by further tuning the steps in **linear annealed policy** because this agent takes many more steps to train. However, the values chosen for CartPole seem to work pretty well enough, so that's an exercise left to the reader.

Agent

The Lunar Lander DQNAgent is again the same, with the exception of a much smaller learning rate, as you can see from the following code:

```
dqn = DQNAgent(model=model, nb_actions=num_actions, memory=memory,
nb_steps_warmup=10, target_model_update=1e-2, policy=policy)
dqn.compile(Adam(lr=0.00025), metrics=['mae'])
```

Training

As you train this agent, you'll notice that the first thing it learns to do is hover the lander, and avoid landing. When the lander finally lands, it receives a very strong reward, either +100 for landing successfully or -100 for crashing. This -100 reward is so strong that the agent would rather incur small penalties for hovering at first. It takes quite a few episodes for our agent to finally get the hint that good landings are better than no landings, because crash landings are so very bad.

 It's possible to shape the reward signal to help the agent learn faster, but doing so is outside of the scope of this book. For more information, check out reward shaping.

Because of this extreme negative feedback for crash landings, it will take the network quite a while to learn to land. Here we are running half a million training steps to get our message across. We will use the following code to train the agent:

```
callbacks = build_callbacks(ENV_NAME)

dqn.fit(env, nb_steps=1000000,
        visualize=False,
        verbose=2,
        callbacks=callbacks)
```

You might be able to further improve this example by tuning the parameter gamma, which defaults to 0.99. If you recall from the Q function, this parameter reduces or increases the impact of future rewards within the Q function.

Results

I've included weights for the Lunar Lander in the chapter Git, and created a script that runs those weights with visualization turned on called `dqn_lunar_lander_test.py`. It loads the trained model weights and runs for 10 episodes. Most of the time, the agent is able to land the Lunar Lander on it's landing pad with surprising skill and accuracy, as you can see in the following screenshot:

Hopefully, this example demonstrates that while deep Q networks aren't quite *rocket science*, they can be used to control a rocket.

Summary

Stanford teaches an entire course only on reinforcement learning. It would have been possible to write an entire book just on reinforcement learning, and in fact that has been done many times. My hope for this chapter is to show you just enough to start you on your way towards solving reinforcement learning problems.

As I solved the Lunar Lander problem, it was easy to let my mind wander from toy problems to actual space exploration with deep Q network-powered agents. I hope this chapter does the same for you.

In the next chapter, I'll show you one last use of Deep Neural networks where we will look at networks that can generate new images, data points, and and even music, called **Generative Adversarial Networks**.

13
Generative Adversarial Networks

While I've spent much of this book talking about networks that classify or estimate, in this chapter I get to show you some deep neural networks that have the ability to create. The **Generative Adversarial Network** (**GAN**), learns to do this through a sort of internal competition between two deep networks, which we will talk about next. In the case of **Deep Convolutional General Adversarial Networks** (**DCGAN**), which is the type of GAN I'm going to focus on in this chapter, the network learns to create images that resemble the images in the training dataset.

We will cover the following topics in this chapter:

- An overview of the GAN
- Deep Convolutional GAN architecture
- How GANs can fail
- Safe choices for a GAN
- Generating MNIST images using a Keras GAN
- Generating CIFAR-10 images using a Keras GAN

An overview of the GAN

Generative Adversarial Networks are all about generating new content. GANs are capable of learning some distribution and creating a new sample from that distribution. That sample might just be a new point on a line that isn't present in our training data, but it could also be a new point in a very complex dataset. GANs have been used to generate new music, sounds, and images. According to Yann LeCun, *adversarial training is the coolest thing since sliced bread* (`https://www.quora.com/session/Yann-LeCun/1`). I'm not sure that sliced bread is especially cool, but Yann LeCun is a very cool guy so I'll take his word for it. Regardless, GANs are incredibly popular and while perhaps not as practical as some of the other topics we've covered in a business setting yet, they deserve some consideration in our survey of deep learning techniques.

In 2014, Ian Goodfellow et al. wrote a paper called **Generative Adversarial Nets** (`https://arxiv.org/pdf/1406.2661.pdf`) that proposed a framework that used the adversarial training of two deep networks, each trying to defeat the other. This framework is composed of two separate networks: a discriminator and a generator.

The discriminator is looking at real data from a training set and fake data from the generator. It's job is to classify each as incoming instance of data as either real or fake.

The generator attempts to fool the discriminator into thinking the data it is generating is real.

The generator and the discriminator are locked into a game where they each try to outsmart the other. This competition drives each network to improve until eventually the output of the generator is indistinguishable from the data in the training set, by the discriminator. When both the generator and discriminator are configured correctly they arrive at a Nash equilibrium where both are unable to find an advantage over the other.

Deep Convolutional GAN architecture

There are many papers on GANs, each proposing new novel architectures and tweaks; however, most of them are at least somewhat based on the **Deep Convolutional GAN (DCGAN)**. For the rest of the chapter, we will be focusing on this model because this knowledge will hopefully serve you well as you take on new and exciting GAN architectures that aren't covered here, such as the **Conditional GAN (cGAN)**, the Stack GAN, the InfoGAN, or the Wasserstein GAN, or possibly some other new variant that you might choose to look at next.

The DCGAN was introduced by Alex Radford, Luke Metz, and Soumith Chintala in the paper *Unsupervised Representation Learning with Deep Convolutional Generative Adversarial Networks* (`https://arxiv.org/pdf/1511.06434.pdf`).

Lets take a look at the overall architecture of the DCGAN next.

Adversarial training architecture

The overall architecture of the GAN is shown in the following figure. The generator and discriminator, which are each separate deep neural networks, are oversimplified as a black box for the sake of easy consumption. We will get to their individual architectures shortly, but first I want to focus on how they interact:

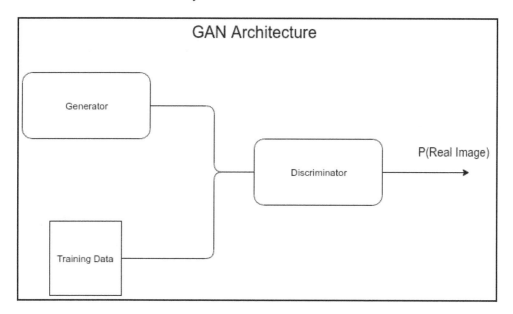

The generator is given a vector of random noise (z) and creates an output *G(z)* (an image in the case of a DCGAN) that it hopes will trick the discriminator.

The discriminator is given both real training data (*X*) and generator output *G(z)*. It's job is to determine the probability that it's input is actually real *P(X)*.

The discriminator and generator are both trained together, in a stack. As one improves, the other also improves until hopefully the generator produces such good output that the discriminator is no longer able to identify the difference between that output and the training data.

Of course, there are a few more details we should cover before you'll be ready to build your own GAN. Next, let's take a deeper look at the generator.

Generator architecture

In this example, we're using layer sizes that are appropriate for generating a *28 x 28* grayscale image, which is exactly what we will be doing later in our MNIST example. The arithmetic of generators can be a little tricky if you haven't worked with one before, so we will cover that as we walk through each layer. The following figure shows the architecture:

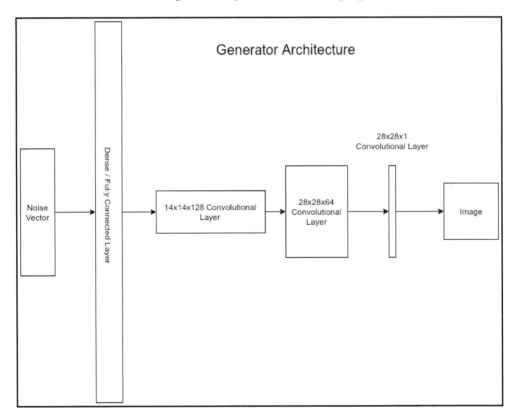

The input to the generator is just a 100 x 1 vector of randomness that we will call a noise vector. GANs tend to work best when this noise vector is generated from a normal distribution.

The first layer of the network is dense and fully connected. It provides us with a way to set up the linear algebra so that we end up with the right shape of output. For each convolutional block, we will end up doubling our first and second axis (the rows and columns that will eventually become the height and width of the image), while the number of channels gradually shrinks to 1. We eventually need the height and width of the output to be 28. So, we will need to start with a *7 x 7 x 128* tensor, so that it can move to *14 x 14* and then eventually *28 x 28*. To accomplish this, we will size the dense layer as *128 x 7 x 7* neurons or 6,272 units. This allows us to reshape the output of the dense layer to *7 x 7 x 128*. If this seems a little less than obvious now, don't worry, it will make sense after you code it.

After the fully connected layer, things are more straightforward. We're using convolutional layers, just like we always have. However, this time we're using them backwards. We're no longer using max pooling to down sample. Instead we're up-sampling, using the convolutions to build up our network as we learn visual features, and eventually outputting a tensor of the appropriate shape.

Typically, the activation of the last layer in the generator is the hyperbolic tangent and the elements within the training image matrices are normalized to be between -1 and 1. This is one of the many GAN hacks that I'll mention throughout the chapter. Researchers have discovered several hacks that have been empirically observed to help build stable GANs, most of which can be found on this Git by Soumith Chintala, who also happens to be one of the authors of the original DCGAN paper at `https://github.com/soumith/ganhacks`. The world of deep learning research is most certainly a small one.

Discriminator architecture

The discriminator's architecture is much more like what we've already seen in previous chapters. It's really just a typical image classifier, as shown in the following figure. The output is sigmoid because the discriminator will be predicting the probability that the input image is a member of the set of real images. The discriminator is solving a binary classification problem:

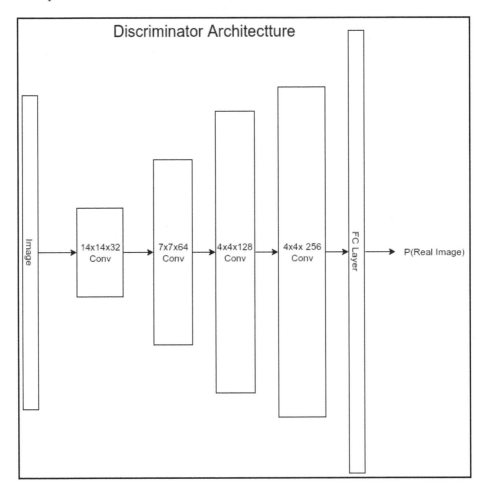

Now that we've covered the architecture of the DCGAN and it's various layers, lets take a look at how the framework is trained.

Stacked training

The DCGAN framework is trained using minibatches, the same way I have previously trained networks in this book. However, later on when we build the code you will notice that we're building a training loop that explicitly controls what happens for each update batch, rather than just calling the `models.fit()` method and relying on Keras to handle it for us. I'm doing this because GAN training requires several models to update their weights over the same batch, so it's slightly more complicated than a single parameter update as we were previously doing.

Training a DCGAN happens in two steps, for each batch.

Step 1 – train the discriminator

The first step in batch training a DCGAN is to train the discriminator on both real data and generated data. The label given to real data will obviously be `1` and the label for fake data is `0`.

Step 2 – train the stack

After the discriminator has updated it's weights, we will train both the discriminator and generator together as a single model. When doing so, we will make the discriminator's weights non-trainable, freezing them in place but still allowing the discriminator to reverse propagate a gradient to the generator so that the generator can update it's weights.

For this step in the training process, we will use a noise vector as input, which will cause an image to be generated by the generator. The discriminator will be shown that image and asked to predict if the image is real or not. The following diagram illustrates this process:

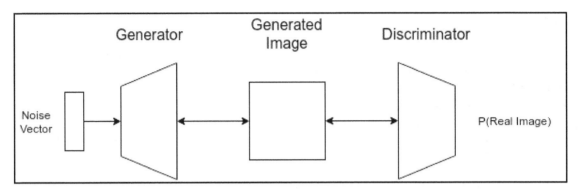

The discriminator will come up with some prediction, which we can call $\hat{y}$. The loss function for this stack will be binary cross-entropy and we will pass the loss function a label of 1, which we can consider y. As you likely recall from earlier in the book, the loss between y and $\hat{y}$ is converted into a gradient that is passed back through the discriminator to the generator. This will update the generator weights, allowing it to benefit from the discriminator's knowledge of the problem space so that it can learn to create a more realistic generated image.

These two steps are then repeated over and over again, hopefully until the generator is able to create data that resembles the data in the training set to a point where the discriminator can no longer tell the two datasets apart and it becomes a guessing game for the discriminator. At this same point, the generator will no longer be able to improve. When we've found this Nash equilibrium, the network is trained.

How GANs can fail

Training a GAN is a tricky thing, to say the least. There are an amazing number of ways one fail at training a GAN. In fact, in writing this chapter, I found myself expanding the vocabulary of my profanity vector significantly while also spending a small fortune on cloud GPU time! Before I show you two working GANs later in the chapter, let's consider what could break and how we might be able to fix those things.

Stability

Training a GAN requires a careful balancing act between the discriminator and generator. The discriminator and generator are both fighting against each other for deep network supremacy. On the other hand, they also need each other to learn and grow. In order for this to work, neither can overpower the other one.

In an unstable GAN, the discriminator might overpower the generator, and become absolutely certain that the generator is fake. The loss goes to zero, and there is no gradient available to be sent to the generator, so it can no longer improve. Game over for the network. The best way to address this is to lower the learning rate of the discriminator. You might also try reducing the number of neurons in the overall discriminator architecture; however, you might miss those neurons later in the training process. Ultimately, tweaking network architectures and hyperparameters is the best way to avoid this situation.

Of course, it might be the other way around, as is the case in mode collapse.

Mode collapse

Mode collapse is a similar and related way for GANs to fail. In mode collapse, the generator learns one mode in a multi-modal distribution and chooses to always use that method to exploit the discriminator. If your training set has fish and kittens in it, and your generator only generates weird kittens and no fish then you've experienced mode collapse. In this case, increasing the power of your discriminator might help.

Safe choices for GAN

I've previously mentioned Soumith Chintala's GAN hacks Git (`https://github.com/soumith/ganhacks`), which is an excellent place to start when you're trying to make your GAN stable. Now that we've talked about how difficult it can be to train a stable GAN, let's talk about some of the safe choices that will likely help you succeed that you can find there. While there are quite a few hacks out there, here are my top recommendations that haven't been covered already in the chapter:

- **Batch norm**: When using batch normalization, construct different minibatches for both real and fake data and make the updates separately.
- **Leaky ReLU**: Leaky ReLU is a variation of the ReLU activation function. Recall the the ReLU function is $f(x) = max(0, x)$.

Leaky ReLU, however, is formulated as:

$$f(x) = \begin{cases} x \ when \ x >= 0 \\ \alpha * x \ when \ x < 0 \end{cases}$$

Leaky ReLU allows very small, non-zero gradients when the unit isn't active. This combats vanishing gradients, which are always a problem when we stack many layers on top of each other like we are in the combination of the discriminator and generator.

- **Use dropout in the generator**: This will provide noise and protect from mode collapse.
- **Use soft labels**: Use labels between 0.7 and 1 for real examples and between 0 and 0.3 for fake examples. This noise helps keep information flowing from the discriminator to the generator.

There are quite a few other GAN hacks available that we cover elsewhere in this chapter; however, I consider these few hacks to be the most important when implementing a successful GAN.

Generating MNIST images using a Keras GAN

We've worked with MNIST before, but this time we will be generating new MNIST like images with a GAN. It can take a very long time to train a GAN; however, this problem is small enough that it can be run on most laptops in a few hours, which makes it a great example. Later we will expand this example to CIFAR-10 images.

The network architecture that I'm using here has been found by, and optimized by, many folks, including the authors of the DCGAN paper and people like Erik Linder-Norén, who's excellent collection of GAN implementations called **Keras GAN** (https://github.com/eriklindernoren/Keras-GAN) served as the basis of the code I used here. If you're wondering how I came to the architecture choices I used here, these are the giants whose shoulders I'm attempting to stand upon.

Loading the dataset

The MNIST dataset consists of 60,000 hand-drawn numbers, 0 to 9. Keras provides us with a built-in loader that splits it into 50,000 training images and 10,000 test images. We will use the following code to load the dataset:

```
from keras.datasets import mnist

def load_data():
    (X_train, _), (_, _) = mnist.load_data()
    X_train = (X_train.astype(np.float32) - 127.5) / 127.5
    X_train = np.expand_dims(X_train, axis=3)
    return X_train
```

As you probably noticed, I'm not returning any of the labels or the testing dataset. I'm only going to use the training dataset. The labels aren't needed because the only labels I will be using are *0* for fake and *1* for real. These are real images, so they will all be assigned a label of 1 at the discriminator.

Building the generator

The generator uses a few new layers that we will talk about in this section. First, take a chance to skim through the following code:

```
def build_generator(noise_shape=(100,)):
    input = Input(noise_shape)
    x = Dense(128 * 7 * 7, activation="relu")(input)
    x = Reshape((7, 7, 128))(x)
    x = BatchNormalization(momentum=0.8)(x)
    x = UpSampling2D()(x)
    x = Conv2D(128, kernel_size=3, padding="same")(x)
    x = Activation("relu")(x)
    x = BatchNormalization(momentum=0.8)(x)
    x = UpSampling2D()(x)
    x = Conv2D(64, kernel_size=3, padding="same")(x)
    x = Activation("relu")(x)
    x = BatchNormalization(momentum=0.8)(x)
    x = Conv2D(1, kernel_size=3, padding="same")(x)
    out = Activation("tanh")(x)
    model = Model(input, out)
    print("-- Generator -- ")
    model.summary()
    return model
```

We have not previously used the UpSampling2D layer. This layer will take increases in the rows and columns of the input tensor, leaving the channels unchanged. It does this by repeating the values in the input tensor. By default, it will double the input. If we give an UpSampling2D layer a *7 x 7 x 128* input, it will give us a *14 x 14 x 128* output.

Typically when we build a CNN, we start with an image that is very tall and wide and uses convolutional layers to get a tensor that's very deep but less tall and wide. Here I will do the opposite. I'll use a dense layer and a reshape to start with a *7 x 7 x 128* tensor and then, after doubling it twice, I'll be left with a *28 x 28* tensor. Since I need a grayscale image, I can use a convolutional layer with a single unit to get a *28 x 28 x 1* output.

This sort of generator arithmetic is a little off-putting and can seem awkward at first but after a few painful hours you will get the hang of it!

Building the discriminator

The discriminator is really for the most part the same as any other CNN that I have previously talked about. Of course, there are a few new things that we should talk about. We will use the following code to build the discriminator:

```
def build_discriminator(img_shape):
    input = Input(img_shape)
    x =Conv2D(32, kernel_size=3, strides=2, padding="same")(input)
    x = LeakyReLU(alpha=0.2)(x)
    x = Dropout(0.25)(x)
    x = Conv2D(64, kernel_size=3, strides=2, padding="same")(x)
    x = ZeroPadding2D(padding=((0, 1), (0, 1)))(x)
    x = (LeakyReLU(alpha=0.2))(x)
    x = Dropout(0.25)(x)
    x = BatchNormalization(momentum=0.8)(x)
    x = Conv2D(128, kernel_size=3, strides=2, padding="same")(x)
    x = LeakyReLU(alpha=0.2)(x)
    x = Dropout(0.25)(x)
    x = BatchNormalization(momentum=0.8)(x)
    x = Conv2D(256, kernel_size=3, strides=1, padding="same")(x)
    x = LeakyReLU(alpha=0.2)(x)
    x = Dropout(0.25)(x)
    x = Flatten()(x)
    out = Dense(1, activation='sigmoid')(x)

    model = Model(input, out)
    print("-- Discriminator -- ")
    model.summary()
    return model
```

First you might notice the oddly shaped `zeroPadding2D()` layer. After the second convolution, our tensor has gone from *28 x 28 x 3 to 7 x 7 x 64*. This layer just gets us back into an even number, adding zeros on one side of both the rows and columns so that our tensor is now *8 x 8 x 64*.

More unusual is the use of both batch normalization and dropout. Typically, these two layers are not used together; however, in the case of GANs, they do seem to benefit the network.

Building the stacked model

Now that we've assembled both the `generator` and the `discriminator`, we need to assemble a third model that is the stack of both models together that we can use for training the generator given the `discriminator` loss.

To do that we can just create a new model, this time using the previous models as layers in the new model, as shown in the following code:

```
discriminator = build_discriminator(img_shape=(28, 28, 1))
generator = build_generator()

z = Input(shape=(100,))
img = generator(z)
discriminator.trainable = False
real = discriminator(img)
combined = Model(z, real)
```

Notice that we're setting the discriminator's training attribute to `False` before building the model. This means that for this model we will not be updating the weights of the discriminator during backpropagation. As we mentioned in the *Stacked training* section, we will freeze these weights and only move the generator weights with the stack. The discriminator will be trained separately.

Now that all the models are built, they need to be compiled, as shown in the following code:

```
gen_optimizer = Adam(lr=0.0002, beta_1=0.5)
disc_optimizer = Adam(lr=0.0002, beta_1=0.5)

discriminator.compile(loss='binary_crossentropy',
                      optimizer=disc_optimizer,
                      metrics=['accuracy'])

generator.compile(loss='binary_crossentropy', optimizer=gen_optimizer)
```

```
combined.compile(loss='binary_crossentropy', optimizer=gen_optimizer)
```

If you'll notice, we're creating two custom **Adam optimizers**. This is because many times we will want to change the learning rate for only the discriminator or generator, slowing one or the other down so that we end up with a stable GAN where neither is overpowering the other. You'll also notice that I'm using `beta_1 = 0.5`. This is a recommendation from the original DCGAN paper that I've carried forward and also had success with. A learning rate of 0.0002 is a good place to start as well, and was found in the original DCGAN paper.

The training loop

We have previously had the luxury of calling `.fit()` on our model and letting Keras handle the painful process of breaking the data apart into minibatches and training for us.

Unfortunately, because we need to perform the separate updates for the discriminator and the stacked model together for a single batch we're going to have to do things the old fashioned way, with a few loops. This is how things used to be done all the time, so while it's perhaps a little more work, it does admittedly leave me feeling nostalgic. The following code illustrates the training technique:

```
num_examples = X_train.shape[0]
num_batches = int(num_examples / float(batch_size))
half_batch = int(batch_size / 2)

for epoch in range(epochs + 1):
  for batch in range(num_batches):
      # noise images for the batch
      noise = np.random.normal(0, 1, (half_batch, 100))
      fake_images = generator.predict(noise)
      fake_labels = np.zeros((half_batch, 1))
      # real images for batch
      idx = np.random.randint(0, X_train.shape[0], half_batch)
      real_images = X_train[idx]
      real_labels = np.ones((half_batch, 1))
      # Train the discriminator (real classified as ones and
      generated as zeros)
      d_loss_real = discriminator.train_on_batch(real_images,
        real_labels)
      d_loss_fake = discriminator.train_on_batch(fake_images,
        fake_labels)
      d_loss = 0.5 * np.add(d_loss_real, d_loss_fake)
      noise = np.random.normal(0, 1, (batch_size, 100))
      # Train the generator
```

```
g_loss = combined.train_on_batch(noise, np.ones((batch_size, 1)))
    # Plot the progress
print("Epoch %d Batch %d/%d [D loss: %f, acc.: %.2f%%] [G loss:
    %f]" %
(epoch,batch, num_batches, d_loss[0], 100 * d_loss[1], g_loss))
    if batch % 50 == 0:
        save_imgs(generator, epoch, batch)
```

There is a lot going on here, to be sure. As before, let's break it down block by block. First, let's see the code to generate noise vectors:

```
noise = np.random.normal(0, 1, (half_batch, 100))
fake_images = generator.predict(noise)
fake_labels = np.zeros((half_batch, 1))
```

This code is generating a matrix of noise vectors (which we've previously called **z**) and sending it to the generator. It's getting a set of generated images back, which I'm calling fake images. We will use these to train the discriminator, so the labels we want to use are 0s, indicating that these are in fact generated images.

Note that the shape here is `half_batch` *x 28 x 28 x 1*. The `half_batch` is exactly what you think it is. We're creating half a batch of generated images because the other half of the batch will be real data, which we will assemble next. To get our real images, we will generate a random set of indices across `X_train` and use that slice of `X_train` as our real images, as shown in the following code:

```
idx = np.random.randint(0, X_train.shape[0], half_batch)
real_images = X_train[idx]
real_labels = np.ones((half_batch, 1))
```

 Yes, we are sampling with replacement in this case. It does work out but it's probably not the best way to implement minibatch training. It is, however, probably the easiest and most common.

Since we are using these images to train the discriminator, and because they are real images, we will assign them *1s* as labels, rather than *0s*. Now that we have our discriminator training set assembled, we will update the discriminator. Also note that we aren't using the soft labels that we had discussed previously. That's because I wanted to keep things as easy as they can be to understand. Luckily the network doesn't require them in this case. We will use the following code to to train the discriminator:

```
# Train the discriminator (real classified as ones and generated as zeros)
d_loss_real = discriminator.train_on_batch(real_images, real_labels)
d_loss_fake = discriminator.train_on_batch(fake_images, fake_labels)
```

```
d_loss = 0.5 * np.add(d_loss_real, d_loss_fake)
```

Notice that here I'm using the discriminator's `train_on_batch()` method. This is the first time I've used this method in the book. The `train_on_batch()` method does exactly one round of forward and backwards propagation. Every time we call it, it updates the model once from the model's previous state.

Also notice that I'm making the update for the real images and fake images separately. This is advice that is given on the GAN hack Git I had previously referenced in the *Generator architecture* section. Especially in the early stages of training, when real images and fake images are from radically different distributions, batch normalization will cause problems with training if we were to put both sets of data in the same update.

Now that the discriminator has been updated, it's time to update the generator. This is done indirectly by updating the combined stack, as shown in the following code:

```
noise = np.random.normal(0, 1, (batch_size, 100))
g_loss = combined.train_on_batch(noise, np.ones((batch_size, 1)))
```

To update the combined model, we create a new noise matrix, and this time it will be as large as the entire batch. We will use that as an input to the stack, which will cause the generator to generate an image and the discriminator to evaluate that image. Finally, we will use the label of 1 because we want to back propagate the error between a real image and the generated image.

Lastly, the training loop reports the discriminator and generator loss at the `epoch/batch` and then, every 50 batches, of every `epoch` we will use `save_imgs` to generate example images and save them to disk, as shown in the following code:

```
print("Epoch %d Batch %d/%d [D loss: %f, acc.: %.2f%%] [G loss: %f]" %
      (epoch,batch, num_batches, d_loss[0], 100 * d_loss[1], g_loss))

if batch % 50 == 0:
    save_imgs(generator, epoch, batch)
```

The `save_imgs` function uses the generator to create images as we go, so we can see the fruits of our labor. We will use the following code to define `save_imgs`:

```
def save_imgs(generator, epoch, batch):
    r, c = 5, 5
    noise = np.random.normal(0, 1, (r * c, 100))
    gen_imgs = generator.predict(noise)
    gen_imgs = 0.5 * gen_imgs + 0.5

    fig, axs = plt.subplots(r, c)
```

```
    cnt = 0
    for i in range(r):
for j in range(c):
            axs[i, j].imshow(gen_imgs[cnt, :, :, 0], cmap='gray')
            axs[i, j].axis('off')
            cnt += 1
    fig.savefig("images/mnist_%d_%d.png" % (epoch, batch))
    plt.close()
```

It uses only the generator by creating a noise matrix and retrieving an image matrix in return. Then, using matplotlib.pyplot, it saves those images to disk in a *5 x 5* grid.

Model evaluation

Good is somewhat subjective, when you're building a deep neural network to create images. Let's take a look at a few examples of the training process, so you can see for yourself how the GAN begins to learn to generate MNIST.

Here's the network at the very first batch of the very first epoch. Clearly, the generator doesn't really know anything about generating MNIST at this point; it's just noise, as shown in the following image:

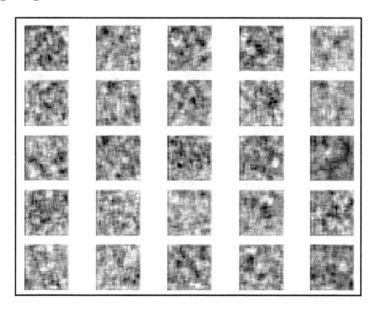

But just 50 batches in, something is happening, as you can see from the following image:

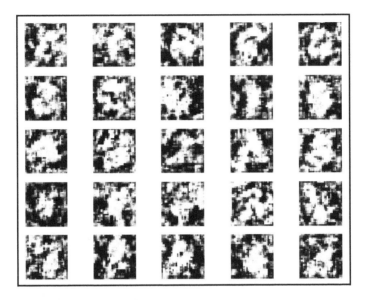

And after 200 batches of epoch 0 we can almost see numbers, as you can see from the following image:

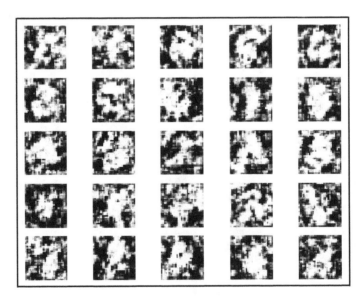

And here's our generator after one full epoch. I think these generated numbers look pretty good, and I can see how the discriminator might be fooled by them. At this point, we could probably continue to improve a little bit, but it looks like our GAN has worked as the computer is generating some pretty convincing MNIST digits, as shown in the following image:

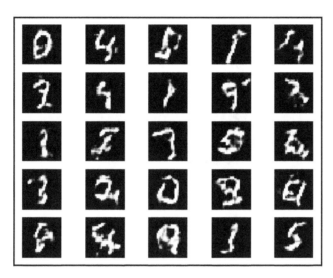

While most of the code will be the same, before we close out the chapter let's look at one more example, using color images.

Generating CIFAR-10 images using a Keras GAN

While the network architecture remains for the most part unchanged I felt it necessary to show you an example that uses color images, as well as providing the example in Git, so that you had some place to start if you wanted to apply a GAN to your own data.

The CIFAR-10 is a famous dataset comprised of 60,000 *32 x 32 x 3* RGB color images, distributed across 10 categories. Those categories are airplanes, cars, birds, cats, deer, dogs, frogs, horses, ships, and trucks. Hopefully, when you see the generated images later, you might see something that you can imagine looks like those objects.

Loading CIFAR-10

Loading the dataset is almost exactly the same, as Keras also provides a loader for CIFAR-10, using the following code:

```
from keras.datasets import cifar10
def load_data():
  (X_train, y_train), (X_test, y_test) = cifar10.load_data()
  X_train = (X_train.astype(np.float32) - 127.5) / 127.5
  return X_train
```

Building the generator

The generator needs to produce *32 x 32 x 3* images. This requires two slight changes to our network architecture that you can see here:

```
input = Input(noise_shape)
x = Dense(128 * 8 * 8, activation="relu")(input)
x = Reshape((8, 8, 128))(x)
x = BatchNormalization(momentum=0.8)(x)
x = UpSampling2D()(x)
x = Conv2D(128, kernel_size=3, padding="same")(x)
x = Activation("relu")(x)
x = BatchNormalization(momentum=0.8)(x)
x = UpSampling2D()(x)
x = Conv2D(64, kernel_size=3, padding="same")(x)
x = Activation("relu")(x)
x = BatchNormalization(momentum=0.8)(x)
x = Conv2D(3, kernel_size=3, padding="same")(x)
out = Activation("tanh")(x)
model = Model(input, out)
```

Since we need to end at 32, and we will upsample twice, we should begin at 8. This is easily accomplished by changing the dense layer and it's respective reshape layer from *128 * 7 * 7* to *128 * 8 * 8*.

Since our image now contains three channels, the last convolutional layer needs to also contain three channels instead of one. That's all there is to it; we can now generate color images!

Building the discriminator

The discriminator is almost completely unchanged. The input layer needs to change from *28 x 28 x 1* to *32 x 32 x 3*. Also the `ZeroPadding2D` can be removed without issue because the layer arithmatic works without it.

The training loop

The training loop remains unchanged, with the exception of the discriminator build call, which requires new dimensions that correspond to CIFAR-10's image size, as shown in the following code:

```
discriminator = build_discriminator(img_shape=(32, 32, 3))
```

 It would often be the case that we would need to adapt our learning rates, or the network architecture, when moving from one dataset to the other; luckily, that's not the case in this example.

Model evaluation

The `CIFAR-10` dataset is certainly more complicated and the network has quite a few more parameters. As such, things are going to take longer. Here's what our images look like on epoch 0, batch 300:

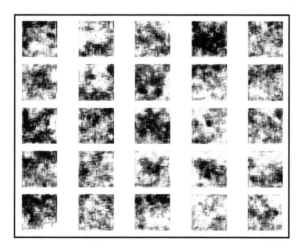

I'm starting to maybe see some edges, but it doesn't really look like anything. If we wait a few epochs though, we're clearly in fuzzy squirrel and weird fish territory. We can see something taking shape, it's just all a little fuzzy, as shown in the following image:

The following image shows our generator after 12 epochs:

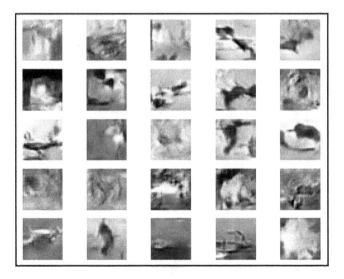

I see very low resolution birds, fish, and maybe an airplane and a truck. We have a long way to go of course, but our network has learned to create images, and that's pretty exciting.

Summary

In this chapter, we looked at GANs and how they can be used to generate new images. We learned a few rules for building GANs well, and we even learned to simulate MNIST and CIFAR-10 images. There is no doubt that you've probably seen some amazing images, created by GANs, in the media. After reading this chapter and working through these examples, you have the tools to do the same. I hope that you can take these ideas and adapt them. The only limitations left are your own imagination, your data, and your GPU budget.

In this book we covered a great many applications of deep learning, from simple regression to Generative Adversarial Networks. My greatest hope for this book is that it might help you make practical use of deep learning techniques, many of which have existed in the domain of academia and research, outside the reach of the practicing data scientist or machine learning engineer. Along the way I hope I might have given you some advice on how to build better deep neural networks, and when to use a deep network as opposed to a more traditional model. If you've followed along with me through out these 13 chapters, thank you for you reading.

> *"We are all apprentices in a craft where no one ever becomes a master."*
> *- Ernest Hemingway*

Other Books You May Enjoy

If you enjoyed this book, you may be interested in these other books by Packt:

TensorFlow 1.x Deep Learning Cookbook
Antonio Gulli, Amita Kapoor

ISBN: 978-1-78829-359-4

- Install TensorFlow and use it for CPU and GPU operations
- Implement DNNs and apply them to solve different AI-driven problems.
- Leverage different data sets such as MNIST, CIFAR-10, and Youtube8m with TensorFlow and learn how to access and use them in your code.
- Use TensorBoard to understand neural network architectures, optimize the learning process, and peek inside the neural network black box.
- Use different regression techniques for prediction and classification problems
- Build single and multilayer perceptrons in TensorFlow

Deep Learning with Keras
Antonio Gulli, Sujit Pal

ISBN: 978-1-78712-842-2

- Optimize step-by-step functions on a large neural network using the Backpropagation Algorithm
- Fine-tune a neural network to improve the quality of results
- Use deep learning for image and audio processing
- Use **Recursive Neural Tensor Networks** (**RNTNs**) to outperform standard word embedding in special cases
- Identify problems for which **Recurrent Neural Network** (**RNN**) solutions are suitable
- Explore the process required to implement Autoencoders
- Evolve a deep neural network using reinforcement learning

Leave a review - let other readers know what you think

Please share your thoughts on this book with others by leaving a review on the site that you bought it from. If you purchased the book from Amazon, please leave us an honest review on this book's Amazon page. This is vital so that other potential readers can see and use your unbiased opinion to make purchasing decisions, we can understand what our customers think about our products, and our authors can see your feedback on the title that they have worked with Packt to create. It will only take a few minutes of your time, but is valuable to other potential customers, our authors, and Packt. Thank you!

Index